D0065578

Say Something

REAL

Humanizing Communication:
Today's Best Business "Strategy"

Lou Solomon
with Patrick McLean

A Book by Lou Solomon
Published by Interact Skills LLC
1435 West Morehead Street
Studio 210
Charlotte, NC 28208

Cover and page design and production by SPARK Publications
www.SPARKpublications.com

Printing History
Edition One, January 2009

ISBN: 978-0-9820349-0-3

Say Something Real
Humanizing Communication:
Today's Best Business "Strategy"

To Sandy,
whose heart and humor
repotted my soul.

AUTHENTIC SPEAKERS

This book would not have been possible without the Authentic Speakers in my life. More than thirty of them are included in this book. I heard these stories live, and while I wish you could do the same—you will recognize the trail of their strength. I have edited some of them for the translation.

In order of appearance:

ACKNOWLEDGEMENTS

To my Interact gypsies: Sally Mitchener, Terri Murphy, Peter Popovich and Patrick Sheehan.

To my book team: Patrick McLean, Fabi Preslar and Mindy Kuhn at SPARK Publications, and Wendy Gill at Professional Communications.

Lifelong thanks to the mentors who have seen something real in me, often when I could not: Charlene Bordonaro, Cynthia Carlson, Kal Kardous, Denny Hammack, Paul Johnson, Gregg Lindahl, June Moore, David Stollmack and Richard Turkheimer.

To my troops: Kyle Caddell, Marilyn Carpenter, Andy Dinkin, Janet England, Judy Hovis, Annemary Lobiondo, Vicky Mitchener, Virginia Popovich, Ellen Ruff, Paige Sheehan, Mary Vickers-Koch, Tom Wright and Joan Wright.

To my coaches who masquerade as clients: Michael Baker, Louis Bledsoe, Jane Cole, Bill England, Jeannie Falknor, Robert Griffin, Judy Kaufman, Yvonne Levine, Sandra Meyer, Chris Mullen, Robert Norris, Roger Pearce, Tim Pettit, Lila Rash, Roger Sarow, David Trotter, Keaven White and Mike Whitehead.

My friends and cohorts: Molly Barker, Amber Brown, Denise Cole, Ann Depta, Nader Elguindi, Valerie Gladden, Marcia Jackson, Linda Kirby, Catherine Little, Cam Marston, Michael Reynolds and Jeff Serenius.

To my creative coaches at the Innovation Institute of the McColl Center for Visual Art: Vicki Taylor and Suzanne Fetscher. To my professors at Queens University at Charlotte: Dr. Kim Gregory and Dr. Will Sparks.

My comrades at Leadership Charlotte: Steve Allen, Derick Close, Martin Grable, Jo Ann Hasskamp, Monica Hamilton, Dave Jenkin, Katie Kaney, Edie Livingstone, Mack McDonald, Elizabeth McKee, Todd Murphy, Jim Rogers, Paul Shipley, Catherine Smith and Tim Newman.

To the fellowship at Hood Hargett Breakfast Club, led by Jenn Snyder and Chuck Hood, and the good that they do for student athletes in our community.

A wink to those who have passed into a state of grace: Dotty Adams, O'Neal Butler, Tom Griscom, Cheryl Hoffman, Paul Franklin and Jody Whitley.

My regrets to anyone with whom I have not been authentic, and my thanks, since I suspect you have been an important teacher to me.

CONTENTS

PREFACE

The future of the American economy demands that we take responsibility for the way we communicate. The ability to inform, to inspire, to spark an idea in the mind of another is what makes us miraculously human. And the more that we use and understand this power, the more human we become. The more we divorce ourselves from Authentic Communication, the less human (and less powerful) we become.

> "There is a vitality, a life force, an energy, a quickening, that is translated through you into action, and because there is only one of you in all of time, this expression is unique. And if you block it, it will never exist through any other medium, and be lost. The world will not have it."
>
> – Martha Graham

Leadership is not an exact or impersonal science. You use what you have. And, for many people, authenticity is the discovery that what they have is more than enough.

I have watched too many executives speak about an organization's vision with crowded slides, and bore everyone in the room. When given encouragement, these same executives can turn off the projector and inspire people by speaking from deep knowledge and humanity—from the head and the heart.

My passion is helping business people speak to one another in a more authentic way. When people take our classes, they speak without slides, canned scripts and business jargon. They speak spontaneously, without notes or a lectern. We encourage them to pause and discover the power of silence. Most of all, they tell their stories. Not the facts or timelines of their lives, but their stories. Their triumphs and tragedies—the wins and the devastating losses.

If there is one thing you should take away from this book, it is this: the world doesn't need you to fit into anything but your own skin. What we need today is not only your deep knowledge, but your experience, insights and stories of what life has taught you.

TERMS

Authenticity
A quality that is genuine and spontaneous.

Authentic Communication
Communication that allows participants to have genuine and spontaneous experiences. The medium in which individuals innovate and thrive.

Authentic Speaking
Speaking from humility, intention, heart and originality.

Culture of Authentic Communication
The experience of a business (for all who come in contact) that is genuine and spontaneous, and void of Sophisticated Bull.

Inauthentic Speaking
Speaking from fear, competence, facts and busy-ness.

Sophisticated Bull
Complicated and meaningless communication, often stemming from fear, habit and distraction.

Spontaneous
An active quality of the present moment.

SECTION I

YOUR INAUTHENTIC STYLE

We are a collection of roles we play for other people.

On my ninth birthday, I got a bright pink envelope from my Uncle Joe, and a five dollar bill slipped out of the birthday card. Five dollars! When I was nine, that was a fortune.

I rushed outside to share my newfound wealth with my best friend Cindy. I did not hear my father follow me outside. As I waved the bill over my head, my father's voice exploded behind me like a bomb: "Don't brag about your money!" My father lifted me up by one arm and swung me into the house.

Inside, the order was repeated: "Never talk about your money!" Talking about money was crude and impolite. The lesson was direct, immediate and I will never forget it.

Most of us have a pretty good idea of who we should be, and how we should behave. Pieces of this idea come to us from all kinds of sources. Parents, family, friends, clients, teachers and the media—there is no shortage of chefs who want to work in the kitchen of you. And because these people are well-meaning, or in a position of apparent authority, we feel compelled to take their advice. Sometimes we even try to take everyone's advice all at once.

And having something to strive for isn't the problem. The problem is that most of us have been taught to speak from the person we think we should be, rather than who we really are.

—"Hi, Lou, how's business?"

— [My biggest client is going bankrupt.] "Business is good!"

We are comfortable functioning this way, and for a casual exchange between acquaintances on the fly, it's mostly okay. But when it counts, you need to say something real.

Too many times, Sophisticated Bull happens. Our subconscious reads the room and gives us the "right" thing to say. These are the moments in which we think we should be less oddball and more normal; less afraid and more confident; less unnoticed and more popular.

This is not a book about the rules. For every rule, there are great leaders who completely ignore it. In spite of the rules, they communicate wonderfully, powerfully, irresistibly. So to worry about the rules is to play it small. We're after something more. For the purposes of this book, we call that something more "authenticity."

The good news is that authenticity is not something you have to learn. You're born with it. It's who you are. The bad news is that a thick vine of business personae has grown over us like kudzu. We are going to have to work hard at cutting it back.

We begin by noticing the nature of the problem—our unconscious blocks and inauthentic ways of communicating.

Your Inauthentic Style

Block 1: *Speaking from Fear*

Block 2: *Speaking from Competence*

Block 3: *Speaking from Facts*

Block 4: *Speaking from Busy-ness*

BLOCK 1
SPEAKING FROM FEAR

Fear of failure makes business a scary place.

As I looked across the ballroom of a San Francisco hotel, I was thinking about all the hairspray, tight cummerbunds and sequins in the room. It was a big night. The music stopped and the audience focused on the stage. The lights dimmed and the CEO stepped out into the spotlight. "If those of you in the back of the room want to move to the front," he said, "tonight you will have the opportunity to hear from the champions who have made it up here."

I was attending an awards show for excellence in ratings and revenue by broadcasting managers and program directors. Everyone in that room had worked so hard and made a huge sacrifice to be there. But there was a bizarre caste system in the seating chart. The very best performers were seated toward the front of the room and the "lesser best" were seated in the back.

After making his opening statement, the CEO went on to say that while everyone had turned in an extraordinary performance, he needed more for the new fiscal year. "Tonight we take time to celebrate, but tomorrow we get up and do it again—only better and smarter," he said. "We are a fast growth organization, and we are committed to fast growth in each and every one of our properties." The rest of his comments were about pushing for higher ratings to attract the most revenue and not falling short of the mark. Walking out that night, one of my team members grumbled that we had worked too hard to be in the cheap seats.

For the most part, we are using a dusty style of management. Way back in the early part of the last century, old Henri Fayol ran a mining company in France. He came up with a system of organization and control to keep the miners productive and in line.

Organization and control are helpful in the midst of a fire drill. But if we are to nurture creativity, control is not so good. We do lots of talking about innovation—but we don't reward employees for innovation, because there's no time to make mistakes if you're going to make budget.

Authentic Communication asks that we open ourselves up to imperfection. Instead we obsess over how to say we lost money last quarter. We are afraid of disappointing managers, who are afraid of disappointing stockholders. Fear of failure is like a blowtorch to self-conscious communication.

There were not many unique moments on the stage that night. The acceptance speeches by the extra-best were well-intentioned but written to say all the right things. We do the same thing in our boardrooms. We say all the right things. We use company-speak and quote complex and often meaningless mission statements.

The irony is that we never cut through the clutter with Sophisticated Bull. Bosses are listeners, just like everyone else. In spotlight moments it is crucial that we don't cower and blow the opportunity.

In the film "The Pursuit of Happyness," Will Smith is set to interview for an internship at the brokerage firm Dean Witter Reynolds. A victim of circumstances, Smith is late to the interview and arrives without a shirt. When a senior executive asks Will Smith what others will say of him if he hired a man who came to an interview without a shirt, Smith replies, "I would say he must have had very nice pants."

So what does this mean to our CEO and his comments that night? If he had been more aware of who was in the room, he might have talked about the giftedness in the room. He might have told a personal story that would create relevance for everyone in the room. He could have spoken from the heart and expressed his gratitude. He could have put positive feelings in the room. Instead, he made some of these hard-working people fearful that they weren't quite good enough.

> We are powerfully imprisoned by the terms in which we have been conducted to think.
>
> – Buckminster Fuller

Business Ego

Thanks to Sigmund Freud, the word "ego" has been a useful part of our vocabulary since 1933. The ego is our primitive instinct that is always ready to go to the mat for our survival. In a similar way, the calculating business ego comes from a different jungle and is fighting to survive. Just look at the language we use:

- Drop-dead deadline
- You're behind pacing
- You're on probation
- Hostile take-over
- Take a hair cut, lose a bonus
- Go toe-to-toe with them
- Take no prisoners on this one

- Watch your back
- Post-mortem meeting
- Win at all costs
- Make it happen
- Eat what you kill
- Take the bull by the horns
- Kick some butt
- This is not the hill to die on
- Winning is the only thing that matters
- She's a silver-tongued devil
- Never let them see you sweat—if you do, they've got you
- Smelling blood in the water
- Keep your nose to the grindstone
- Play your cards close
- Get your game face on
- Heads will roll if we can't close this case
- Kick 'em to the curb
- You could lose your shirt
- Everything has a price
- Every man for himself
- Keep your friends close, but keep your enemies closer

Alpha Dog Deals

For some of us, our best idea for negotiation is to be cunning and deceitful. We've filled the bookstores with cheesy how-to books that put all the attention on the making the "right" moves, and not enough attention on creating the future. These books seduce us with come-ons like, "How to get people to do what you want." Apparently we need to wear the right suit. Wear our game faces. Sit in the power seat. Speak first. Speak last.

More often than not, we miss the fact that closing gargantuan deals requires raw brainpower—and integrity—to get invited to the table in the first place.

As business brains evolve, we are realizing that great negotiation takes genuinely smart people. Bruce Wasserstein is the CEO of Lazard and recipient of the Harvard Law School Great Negotiator Award. He has helped broker over a thousand deals worth hundreds of billions of dollars. He defines his approach as trustworthy, creative, smart and focused on creating the future for both parties.

It is mere myth that great negotiators are poker-faced and aloof. After all, who can trust a man or woman without a pulse? Executives who display a lack of emotion are less likely to preserve valuable business relationships, gain concessions and persuade others, according to a study in the *Journal of Organizational Behavior and Human Decision Processes*. Wringing the life out of your face is not a successful tactic.

When we speak about what is really important to us, there is energy in the room. What happens when a professional lets you see the side of him that cares deeply about his father? He cuts through the ambient noise in the room and earns your trust.

> Dialogue is a way of understanding that two realities can exist side by side. This takes brains, not dominance.

"Murphy" Unedited
David M. Schilli

"My dad goes by 'Murphy' and that's the name on the speed dial of my cell phone. He was born in St. Genevieve, Missouri—a small, rural town—in 1934. He was born in a two-room house. His father owned a truck and ran vegetables and other produce.

This was my father's humble beginning. He has been without a doubt one of the biggest influences in my life. I've had a lot of occasions to think about that lately, because he is having a serious operation.

It never dawned on me how much he means to me. The older I get, the more I realize I'm a lot like him. He's intensely private. And those people who know me would say that I am the same way. He's unfailingly loyal. I hope I am the same way.

My dad is a simple man. He has a great sense of humor. He's real. Some of the best memories of spending time with him are just doing the simple things. I can remember when I was away at school and would come home—in 24 hours we would have the cleanest cars. Because that was the way we would spend time and connect. We would wash cars.

My dad worked very, very hard. But, he was all about quality, not quantity. I've probably been less of a son to him than he would have liked. But over the last few weeks we have talked more on the phone and connected more than we have since I was away at college. It was from those humble beginnings that he has done himself proud. I only hope his son can do the same."

Speaking from Fear

To take our informal assessment, simply reflect on each statement. Determine which of the three statements you relate with most, and the intensity of that connection.

1. Fear of authority: When I'm in the boardroom, I am playing to the CEO.

1	2 3 4 5	6 7 8
The decision maker in the room is the one who counts.	I don't play exclusively to the boss, but of course I skew my comments.	I have a candid conversation with everyone in the room.

2. Negotiation: Truthfully I am less interested in both sides getting what they want, and more interested in getting what I need.

1	2 3 4 5	6 7 8
It's only natural.	It's nice if everyone is happy when it's over.	I want to participate in the challenge of creating a great future.

3. Self-doubt: I don't like asking questions, and before I offer comments, I want to have my information down pat.

1	2 3 4 5	6 7 8
I feel insecure if others know more than I do.	I don't mind asking questions of my teammates—but not when management is in the room.	I learn by asking questions. I don't know everything.

4. Leveraging authority: When performance is off, I come down on my troops.

1	2 3 4 5	6 7 8
What else would you do?	This is necessary at times but it doesn't work if you do it all the time.	I ask them what they think we should do.

5. Fear of exposure: I am hesitant to share my mistakes.

1	2 3 4 5	6 7 8
Why give people something to use against you?	I can tell my friends at work but I don't put them out there for everyone.	We all learn by failing. I don't mind sharing my mistakes.

Inauthentic Speaking 5-15
Fear still holds you back 16-25
Authentic Speaking 26-40

BLOCK 2
SPEAKING FROM COMPETENCE

We are afraid of the struggle involved in learning
a new activity. We trust ourselves less and less.

I stood in line with my mother to register for swimming lessons at Andrews
Air Force Base. The diving board thumped as divers hit the water. The
place was a beehive of kids and towels. Realizing I was about to be in a
class with strangers, I began to panic. I got sick to my stomach and wound up
sitting poolside.

I had the same anxiety on the first day of class
at new schools. When the car stopped at the curb, I
wanted to turn around and go back home. I felt lost
and clumsy, until I learned my routes—from the front
door to my home room, from there to the lunch room,
from the lunch room to art class, from art class to my
locker and so on. When I could repeat the obstacle
course I began to feel competent.

No one likes to be the beginner. So we put energy
into achieving a level of competence in the new skill,
and we repeat the process until we get very good at
doing it one way. The problem is that we stop exercising the ability to think newly.

> It is a wrong idea that
> a master is a finished
> person. Finished
> persons are people
> who are closed up,
> quite satisfied that
> there is little or
> nothing more to learn.
>
> – Robert Henri

As long as I stayed the course, I had no shot at learning more about the school.
Businesses that get so good at doing something one way have leaders that resist
change and will tell you, "This is the way we've always done it, " which is the death
knell for innovation.

My first experience with a high-stakes business presentation was in the
mid-80s. I spoke to a group of executives in Miami. I spent a week memorizing the
script. I became a competent presenter in a suit, wearing a very serious face and using
all the right buzz words. It was many years later when I began to drop the idea of
perfection, in the interest of connection.

Crusty presentation skills are a part of unconscious Sophisticated Bull.
Being the center of attention and looking incompetent is the stuff of our
nightmares. It's fine for a youngster to wobble when learning to ride a bike. We
don't ridicule, "Hey—that kid needs training wheels!" But adults often forbid

themselves to return to the place of innocent and natural learning. We stay safe and increasingly inauthentic.

If you want more, trust yourself. Be willing to break down the act of replication. If you're giving safe presentations, there is no brilliance, only competence. That is not to say you aren't using competent skills—but you can become robotic if you stop digging and risking.

Innovation Institute

The Innovation Institute is the brain child of Suzanne Fetscher at the McColl Center for Visual Art in Charlotte, North Carolina. The Institute helps business people "see" from an artist's perspective.

There are six program days at the Institute and each one features an amazing artist. The artist spends an entire day helping you to dig down underneath all of your business competence.

In my class I joined a cadre of bankers, lawyers and architects in aprons. We played with scraps of fabric, threw paint at a large canvas, learned the art of screen printing—and built rooms with scrap material. We were totally and completely outside our comfort zones.

We learned that great artists push themselves to struggle. They know that once they get stuck doing art one way, they have lost the essence of creativity— instead, they are replicating.

We learned that being creative has nothing to do with being artistic. Just because we can sketch what we see doesn't necessarily mean we are creative. A couple of the men in our group who struggled the most were perhaps the most creative.

The Innovation Institute is facilitated by a brilliant creativity coach, Vicki Taylor. Her thoughts on competence have inspired this section.

Starting Over

In 1966 Bob Dylan played the Newport Festival and swapped his acoustic guitar for an electric guitar. He was booed off the stage and called a traitor. His fans felt he was turning his back on "true" folk music—the way folk artists had always done it. Dylan went on to have legendary success with albums such as "Like a Rolling Stone." Since then the Newport event has been called "the night popular music changed forever."

When Tiger Woods changed his swing, most people scratched their heads. Here was a golfer who was the #1 player in the world. So why change? Sports writers say the ideal swing is not fixed. It is ever-evolving and Tiger is leading the way.

People experience a new level of insight and ability by scrapping the old way and learning a new way. Eighteen months after making the changes, Tiger came back to dominate a PGA Tour.

What is the swing you need to break down? The way you think about speaking and presenting? Your philosophy about change?

> **A hero is someone who understands the responsibility that comes with his freedom.**
>
> *– Bob Dylan*

"From Now On" Edited
Ivan Strunin

Ivan Strunin is an accomplished executive, a musician and a father. He tells a story about an encounter with death that changed his life forever.

Ivan was rushed to the hospital with internal bleeding years ago. He was given two transfusions, but was still bleeding. Doctors ran a myriad of tests and couldn't find the problem.

"I began to realize I might never get out of the hospital," says Ivan, "so I began making plans and thinking of what I would tell my kids." Two days later Ivan's doctor announced that he was improving. Ivan began to realize that he would be leaving the hospital to resume his life. He felt complete and utter joy.

"I had a revelation," says Ivan, "This goes back to growing up in a household with immigrant, depression-era parents who were really afraid of the world—afraid of everything."

Ivan explains that this fear caused his parents to stay the course and avoid trying anything different. The answer out of their mouths was always "no." If you say "no" and you don't do it, you will be safe. Ivan said he was raising his children the same way: "My first reaction was to say 'no' to them."

On the last day in the hospital, Ivan decided that from that moment on, he would look for opportunities to say "yes."

"I decided that I wanted to start over and to give my children 'yes' for the rest of their lives. When we bring children into the world, we should find ways to say 'yes.'"

Speaking from Competence

1. Denial: There's no reason to look for ways of doing things differently.		
1	2 3 4 5	6 7 8
If it ain't broke, don't fix it.	I would, but I honestly don't have time.	Let's start from scratch and build something better.

2. Stuck: I always script my presentations and memorize the content.		
1	2 3 4 5	6 7 8
I am not open to doing it differently. It's too risky.	I am working on being more conversational, but I am still uncomfortable with ad-lib moments.	I am prepared but I also want a spontaneous dialogue with listeners.

3. Fear of struggle: I admit I have heard myself say, "This is the way we've always done it."		
1	2 3 4 5	6 7 8
I am only interested in getting through the day—not learning something new.	I am comfortable doing things the way I learned them, but I like a little variety.	Discomfort in learning something new means we're innovating.

4. Fear of criticism: I fear that by trying something new I will be judged by others.		
1	2 3 4 5	6 7 8
My teammates are sharks.	I will try something new if there's not too much at stake.	People respond in kind when you put yourself out there.

5. Status quo: Management isn't asking for Authentic Speaking, so why worry with this at all?		
1	2 3 4 5	6 7 8
I don't need speaking skills in my job.	Management is only interested in a good sales pitch—and I'm not in sales.	I am willing to take a risk with Authentic Communication—to inspire myself and others.

Inauthentic Speaking 5-15
Fear of incompetency still holds you back 16-25
Authentic Speaking 26-40

BLOCK 3
SPEAKING FROM FACTS

Many of us still go for the "safe" presentation by
showing up with facts and no feelings.

In the TV drama Dragnet, Sergeant Joe Friday wanted "Just the facts, m'am." That line captures a core value of the 20th Century.

We work with professionals who feel they are valued for the semi truck of information parked on the left side of their brain. Very smart people who deal with complexity in their work naturally focus on process, sometimes at the exclusion of the heart. That's where the trouble starts. When they focus on the information and "getting it right," they lose the natural energy of conversation.

The spoken word does not travel well on facts alone; relationships are not built upon facts alone. Clients will tell me, "But this is serious business." Serious does not mean boring. But boring can translate into lost relationships.

Recently I was working with a group of gifted professionals, and one of them objected to the use of the word "passion," because he had no intention of coming off like a TV evangelist. We agreed on the substitute phrase, "deep interest."

As the session went on, he began to speak from not only his knowledge but his humanity. He was surprised at his own strength as a communicator. It doesn't matter what you call it, it takes more than the facts for people to connect to you.

Intelligence as a Test Score

We began measuring brain power, or cognitive capacity, over a hundred years ago, when Alfred Binet came up with IQ testing.

I started school in England. When we were stateside again, my mother had me tested for an IQ score before placing me in grade school. It was so mysterious. I sensed I had done well, because she would elude to my score with a smile and a wink. I knew it was important information, but it was un-discussable.

Of course there are many ways to look at intelligence. In *Emotional Intelligence: Why It Can Matter More Than IQ*, Daniel Goleman carved out a new place for business people to consider intelligence—through self-awareness.

Today Goleman is researching the fact that the brain produces "mirror neurons" that come into play in an organization. A leader's actions actually signal others to follow and mirror his or her style of communication. Since being in a good mood promotes performance, the ill-tempered boss is bad for business. It's okay for leaders to be demanding, but if they are approachable with an easy-going tone, leaders will get a lot more done.

The Right Brain

Roger W. Sperry was the biologist who rocked the world with his research in the '60s and '70s. He discovered the right-brain-left-brain dichotomy of the brain. The left brain handles verbal and rational brain thinking; it thinks serially and reduces its thoughts to numbers, letters and words. The right brain is your intuitive, conceptual brain. It thinks in pictures and dabbles in imagination, non-linear thought and the big picture.

We know the brain is far more complicated than two halves of a coconut. But Sperry's model has given us a powerful way to understand the two forms of thought, and the fact that up until this point, education has favored the left brain. Authors like Daniel Pink believe we are entering the Conceptual Age of the right brain.

Jane Goodall

As a young woman in the '70s, I wanted to be Jane Goodall. I saved the copy of *Life Magazine* with her photo on the cover—she was the hippie of the jungle. I thought she had the coolest job in the world. Goodall was a radical in the primate research field. Instead of tagging and numbering animals, she observed personalities and named each individual chimp.

At first Goodall was criticized for soft science, until she proved herself over and over. In '86 she published *The Chimpanzees of Gombe* with enough quantitative research to satisfy the old-line researchers. Her discovery that chimpanzees were using tools turned our knowledge of chimps on its ear. Goodall used both facts and her own observations and understanding of emotion to study the personalities in chimps. This was her genius.

Content Ladder

Here's the good news for gifted people who love new frontiers. There's another ladder of mastery out there. If you don't have a deep understanding of the facts, you're done. No excuses. But greatness lies in weaving that knowledge into your humanity.

Level I	Stand alone, logical facts
Level II	Knowledge and understanding of what the facts mean—and an overview of what is known in your field
Level III	Level II plus: creativity, imagery and stories to produce new relevance for listeners
Level IV	Level III plus: wisdom to value humanitarian concepts and global impact

BLOCK 4
SPEAKING FROM BUSY-NESS

Authenticity requires the time it takes to become curious
and consider what you think about life, in your own words.

Recently I took a short trip to Cincinnati to teach a seminar. I checked email and took phone calls every step of the way. At night I worked on my laptop to prepare for a webinar, while listening to CNN in the background. On break during the seminar I called into a conference call. I checked in at the airport via an automated kiosk. I came home to a hundred emails, a dozen calls, a stack of mail, three newspapers, and an important fax to attend to, recommending a good friend for a position. I got home just in time too. My phone was almost dead.

> We've lost a sense of improvisation and spontaneity...We don't take time to compose original works.
>
> – Max Vengerov

Every day we rush into our office buildings and meet to talk about the need to innovate in order to thrive or even survive in a competitive, global economy. But we can't get out of meetings to do the very thing we're meeting about. So we check our email during meetings to save time. We're so busy, we wind up running half-decent meetings, we make respectable showings at beauty contests and trade shows and we give lackluster presentations like everyone else.

We can't see that we are side-stepping true innovation, which begins with the way we communicate with one another. We might suspect it, but we don't have time to really think about it.

Many of us like to blame technology for our insanity. We even go so far as to say that technology will break our ability to connect face-to-face in a meaningful way. This is Sophisticated Bull. Only we can break that ability. When used for good and without obsession, technology can provide great freedom. We have allowed ourselves to become dazed by technology because it helps feed our busy-ness.

Time

We seem to be running, running, running at the height of distraction. You can hear it in the voices of colleagues. You can see it on the faces of moms who are loading up summer schedules. We are fading away from the present moment into the wallpaper of preoccupation with ourselves.

Authenticity is awareness and it takes the one thing we're not willing to give up: time. It takes time to be authentic because you have to build awareness by paying attention to the interest you have in books, blogs, news stories, industry trades and everything in between. You have to consider what you think about life, in your own words.

> No amount of human having or human doing can make up for a deficit in human being.
>
> – John Adams

We believe we actually don't have time to be interesting. Let's say you are presenting the executive summary for 50 slides. Are you offering any value that goes beyond the slides? What is it? Are you coming out from behind yourself to be candid? Can you tell us what is important to you? Are you peppering in some color that comes from your own curiosity?

"Good Job, Great Job" Unedited
Mick Mixon

Mick Mixon is the play-by-play radio announcer for the Carolina Panthers. He was formerly a color analyst and production manager for the University of North Carolina's "Tar Heel Sports Network", where he was teamed with "The Voice of the Tar Heels", Woody Durham. One of Mick's early career mentors made an impression on him:

"Like most young men at 25, I thought I knew much more than I did. When I was a quarter of a century old, I thought, 'I've got it. I've graduated. I'm making money. I'm having fun. It's just a matter of time before a network snaps me up.'

I wish I had known I was nowhere near as good as I thought I was. And I could have gone on like that, in that maturity vacuum, for a long, long time, if it hadn't been for my news director at WIS Radio in Columbia. His name was Bob McAlister and he respected me enough to tell me something I desperately needed to know.

In April of 1983 my assignment was to go to Hilton Head and cover the Heritage Golf Tournament. My job was to interview the golfers and call in seven reports a day, Wednesday through Sunday. I did that. I thought I did a pretty good job. When I got back that Monday morning, I stopped by Bob McAlister's office and said, 'Hey Bob, how'd you like my reports?' Like an idiot I was actually fishing for a compliment.

Bob said, 'Well, you did a good job. But you didn't do a great job. Would you like to hear how you might have done a great job?' Bob wasn't much of a sports fan, but he knew journalism. He paused for a moment to gather his thoughts and then he spoke: 'Here's what you might have asked: What's it like for the golfers on tour—do they get lonely? What's it like to be a caddy? What is the divorce rate on tour? Is there a fitness trailer? Is there an equipment trailer? How do the local people feel about the tournament? What's the environmental impact from the runoff of fertilizer and pesticides? Mick, you are down there doing your seven reports a day but I'm up here trying to run a radio station. We have news blocks in the morning and in the afternoon. You did your assignment but that was ALL you did.'

I was crushed. I had let him down.

The next week I had the same assignment, for the Master's. I went down in the same news car to do the same series of reports, Wednesday through Sunday. This time I created an electronic blizzard between Augusta and Columbia. I interviewed everybody—the security guard named Tiny, the wives, and the couple that rented their home and left town. When I got back I was one tired son of a gun. On Monday morning I was at my desk typing the 7:45 a.m. news report, and a shadow came over me. It was Bob McAlister. He looked down at me and said, 'Hey Mick—great job at Augusta.'

The lesson for me was simple but perfect. Doing a great job is difficult. Often I fall short. But at least, thanks to Bob McAlister, I know the difference between good and great."

SECTION II

YOUR AUTHENTIC STYLE

We spend most of our lives struggling to gain the credibility that only comes from being who we really are.

In *The Legend of Bagger Vance: A Novel of Golf and the Game of Life*, author Steven Pressfield tells a powerful tale of a man rediscovering his authenticity. The man is Rannulph Junuh, once the pride of Savannah, Georgia, but now a hollow and deeply wounded survivor of World War I. When the book starts Rannulph is dissipated and drinking himself to death. When a great golf match between Walter Hagen and Bobby Jones is organized in Savannah, the town begs Rannulph, once their greatest golfer, to play.

Of course, Junuh refuses. A broken man, he has no faith left in himself. But then comes the advice of the mysterious caddy for whom the book is titled, Bagger Vance:

> *Inside each and every one of us*
> *is our one true authentic swing.*
> *Something that's ours and ours alone.*
> *Something that can't be learned...*
> *something that's got to be remembered.*

Pressfield's book is a powerful fable. And like all fables, it finds a way to tell us a truth that is bigger than any one aspect of the story.

This section is a reminder of the ways in which we release ourselves into authenticity.

Your Authentic Style

Release 1: *Speaking from Humility*

Release 2: *Speaking from Intention*

Release 3: *Speaking from the Heart*

Release 4: *Speaking from Original Thought*

RELEASE 1
SPEAKING FROM HUMILITY

True humility is lost on most of us, because
when it shows up, it looks like confidence.

Americans have had a love affair with the self-esteem and self-help industry for years. But like the diet business, it's a quickie that gets us over a rough spot, and leaves us hungry. It is that gob of cotton candy when what we really need is meat and potatoes and maybe even some lima beans.

We seek self-esteem so we'll feel great about ourselves. Yet researchers have found that when self-esteem is the main goal, relationships are hindered because people become too focused on themselves. The pursuit of self-esteem can make us brittle and nervous. Worst of all, it's the wrong prize.

We don't understand humility. In our secret hearts, don't most of us see humility as a trait belonging to losers who submit to poverty and lowly groveling? How can we possibly be humble and go kick ass in business?

"Big Deal" Edited
Winston Kelley

NASCAR Hall of Fame Director Winston Kelley once told me a story about Richard Petty. Winston was six years old when he met Richard Petty. He recalls tugging on his shirt after he won his first Daytona 500. In the midst of the excitement, Petty looked down and took a moment to acknowledge and speak to the boy. According to Winston, Petty has always been accessible and humble. "He's a big deal, but he doesn't act like it," says Kelley.

Real confidence is not about feeling great about ourselves and being a big deal. It's about knowing that acting like a big deal is completely unnecessary.

The speaker without humility burns up a lot of energy trying to be a big deal, and is recognized as being insecure. A speaker who runs over the allotted time and doesn't understand the audience is perceived as arrogant. People who dominate even a brief conversation are bores.

The attitude behind a talk given by a speaker with humility communicates:

I will tell you what I know from experience, but I don't know everything.
I stand for certain beliefs, but I don't believe I am better than anyone else.
I am interested in what you think.
I am open to consider a new perspective.

"Pure Win" Edited
John Freeman, Jr.

Inexperienced speakers are often the most authentic. Instead of bringing their ego to the front of the room, they bring gratitude, and we love them immediately.

I met NASCAR Busch driver John Freeman, Jr. in the spring of his senior year in high school. He came through one of our courses with people who were twice his age, yet he was comfortable enough to be straightforward and humble.

We asked each participant in the course to bring with them an item that represented a meaningful story. Freeman brought a charred driver's glove. He told us a story about the first time he drove a new car in a new series. He was just testing the car, but found himself running in second position.

Toward the end of the race, Freeman began to get warm. He knew the car was on fire but he kept running. He could feel his shoes melting, but he kept running.

Under a caution flag, the wind stopped blowing through the car and it was engulfed in flames. Freeman unbuckled his harness and dove out of the car unharmed. His crew ran out to him and pushed the car into the infield. They sawed parts of the body off and got it ready to run a couple more laps, just so their driver could get points for finishing the race.

"That was the plan, but I had so much adrenaline from being on fire I went back to the field from 23rd, took the lead on the final lap and won the race," he told us. "I was pushing with everything I had."

"After the race, the car was so black you couldn't see the sponsor logos," he said, "but that win was really meaningful to me. You can always win with a car that's better than the rest. But to win on your own, pushing with everything…that's a win that's pure."

No one but John Freeman, Jr. could have told this story. He created a unique moment in time with those last few words. Everyone in the room knew it.

Many of us worry that our experience is not enough. We worry about saying the right thing and being the perfect version of ourselves. But perfection does not play to authentic communication.

If your talk is void of gratitude and respect for others, we won't care too much about knowing you. If you allow us to see the individual who knows it's not necessary to act like a big deal, we will feel that we already know you well. Say what really matters; say what you believe; share your mistakes; and talk about the astonishing, pure wins.

In *Good to Great*, Jim Collins describes the type of leaders found in companies achieving true greatness as non-celebrity Level 5 leaders. In a nutshell, Level 5 leaders have an unusual combination of intense professional will—and deep personal humility. These leaders credit others, external factors, and good luck for their companies' success—but when results are poor, they blame themselves.

"Sure, I'm Lucky"
Lou Gehrig Excerpt

Lou Gehrig set historic records as a baseball player. He was known as the "Iron Horse," and led the New York Yankees to win nine American League pennants and eight World Series.

Gehrig is best remembered, however, for the words of humility and grace he spoke at Yankee Stadium in July of 1939, less than two years before losing his battle with ALS, today called "Lou Gehrig's Disease." Here are a few lines from that powerful Farewell Speech:

Opening

"Fans, for the past two weeks you have been reading about the bad break I got. Yet today I consider myself the luckiest man on the face of this earth.

I have been in ballparks for seventeen years and have never received anything but kindness and encouragement from you fans. Look at these grand men. Which of you wouldn't consider it the highlight of his career just to associate with them for even one day? Sure I'm lucky."

Closing

"When you have a father and mother who work all their lives so you can have an education and build your body—it's a blessing! When you have a wife who has been a tower of strength and shown more courage than you dreamed existed—that's the finest I know. So I close in saying that I may have had a tough break, but I have an awful lot to live for."

Speaking from Humility

1. Missing it: I'm not interested in developing humility.

1	2 3 4 5	6 7 8
After all, there's that line about a "forced feeding on humble pie."	I know being humble is better than being a blowhard.	Humility is one of my most important goals.

2. Telling versus showing: I am frustrated when people don't seem to know I have credibility.

1	2 3 4 5	6 7 8
Sometimes I do a little name-dropping.	I promote myself but in a tasteful way.	I put energy into connecting with people. Things work out.

3. Fear of exposure: I feel more secure if I don't show weakness.

1	2 3 4 5	6 7 8
Who wants to hear me cry?	I can be vulnerable with some, but not all people at work.	Being vulnerable is a willingness to not be defensive.

4. Pursuing self-esteem: I wish I had more self-esteem.

1	2 3 4 5	6 7 8
I read books about how to feel good about myself.	I work hard. Self-esteem comes from accomplishments.	Real confidence comes from humility.

5. Fear of conflict: I feel threatened if someone voices another opinion.

1	2 3 4 5	6 7 8
I feel flushed and angry.	I'm okay with it if it's a brainstorming session.	I like to hear different viewpoints.

Inauthentic Speaking 5-15
Misunderstanding still holds you back 16-25
Authentic Speaking 26-40

RELEASE 2
SPEAKING FROM INTENTION

Live out of your intention, not your sleep.

S tephen Covey, among others, taught us that there's a gap between stimulus and response, and within that gap you have the power to choose. When someone throws you a barb, instead of flying off the handle, you can pause for a nanosecond and make a better choice.

Ultimately, we should aspire to be martial artists at intentional speaking. To be available in the present moment, and responsible for what we do with it. Everywhere you go, in every conversation, in every presentation, you have an opportunity to *Say Something Real*.

Trouble is, most of us are more like Barney Fifes than martial artists. There is a gravitational pull to be lazy with the gift of language. We say the same things we said yesterday, we make sweeping generalizations and we use Sophisticated Bull. Worse, we blame or gossip about other people. Nearly 90 percent of Americans say they are affected by destructive and hurtful speech.

Practicing that nanosecond pause is a lifetime assignment, so there's no time like the present to begin. This week, when you think of it, eavesdrop on yourself. When you hear yourself make a sweeping statement, think, "Is that really true? Is that what I wanted to say?"

Soon you'll notice that there actually is a gap. It's there, just before you speak. It's there to give you time to choose your intention to speak from humility and not from false self-esteem.

"Intentional Words" Edited
Michael Baker

Michael Baker is a tax partner at an accounting firm—and one of the most passionate human beings I have ever met. He told us a story about meeting his hero, Jim Lovell.

Baker was emceeing an industry event at which he would actually introduce this American Great. He had watched the film, *Apollo 13*, a dozen times. He was going to introduce the man who said, "Houston, we have a problem."

Jim Lovell took the stage and spoke for only 15 minutes. Baker was frustrated. He wanted more from a man he had built up in his mind to be more than human.

The next morning, Baker was included in a breakfast during which Lovell told his story. At one moment the conversation stopped. Someone asked him, "How do you come through that—four or five days, knowing you're probably going to die?"

Lovell answered, "After that experience . . . I am not afraid to live." Baker smiled deeply to himself. Yes. True greatness in just a few words.

Responsibility

We create with our thoughts and our words. Everyone will tell you that they know this is true, but very few of us live like we know it. We're so busy being busy, we forget to participate in the creative process sewn into our words.

After all, intentional speaking is a lot of work. To thoughtfully choose what we say and how we say it; to say what we really believe and mean to say; and to offer something valuable. To take a risk to *Say Something Real*.

This is the work of life. It's entirely possible to cruise through life looking good and saying nothing real. But, great things can't happen when you're cruising. Great things happen when you choose your words and make a stand.

The word *"author"* comes from the Latin word, "auctor," which means the source, creator or originator. The word "authority" is closely related to "author." It comes from the Latin word, "auctoritas," which means freedom from doubt; belief in yourself and that it is that quality that is respected. Natural authority does not control people, it influences people through respect.

Giving pure attention to what we say means we accept the role as author. To make a declaration is to grab the reins of life, to dig down deep into the power of communication instead of skimming the surface.

"Breaking Through" Edited
Nancy McCoy

When we fall on hard times, and all of us do, it's tempting to seek out comfort and pull the cover up. But some of us decide to seek out challenge, so we can overcome feeling small.

Nancy McCoy stepped to the front of the room holding a broken piece of concrete block. She studied it and smiled before she spoke.

Nancy told us that during a hard time in her life, she decided to go the route of challenge. She painted the picture of herself as a woman who was terrified, walking into the Greensboro Academy of Tae Kwon Do. She felt awkward and self-conscious.

As the instructor told her about the programs, she watched children on one side of the room and 20-year-olds on the other. Seeing the pain and distraction on her face, the instructor stopped and asked what she was thinking.

"I can't do this," she said.

The instructor was short in stature but was known for his big heart. Looking up at her, he said, "Never say you cannot do a thing. Never say cannot."

For the next two years, Nancy's instructor allowed her to risk herself. She found the courage to face life and come out the other side, stronger.

Nancy said, "In time I learned to say 'I can do this.'" Holding up the brick, she said, "This is what I was able to accomplish. With one hand and one strike."

"Against the Odds" Edited
Robert B. Norris

I was doing research in the archives of the Charlotte Observer in '02 and came across a college photo of my good friend, Robert Norris. I almost passed over it. He was a bulked-up defensive linebacker for the Davidson Wildcats.

Today Norris is a husband, father and managing partner of a successful law firm. The next time I saw him, I asked him about the photo. "Don't pull that photo out," Norris laughed. Our conversation drifted to his most memorable game.

Davidson was playing East Carolina for the Southern Conference Championship. The game was for the Tangerine Bowl, which is now the Citrus Bowl, in Orlando. "We went there with great expectations," said Norris, "knowing what was at stake, and feeling it was our year to beat East Carolina."

In the first play of the game, the halfback came around Norris and suddenly, he was in the end zone. Within seconds East Carolina had seized the momentum of the game. "By half-time, they had set a record running around me with something like 400 yards rushing," said Norris. "We were behind 27 to 7."

The Wildcats walked back to the locker room with their heads down, while East Carolina students hurled tangerines at their helmets. "It was humiliating," said Norris.

...I believe that this nation should commit itself to achieving the goal, before this decade is out, of landing a man on the moon and returning him safely to the earth.

– President John F. Kennedy, Joint session of Congress, May 25, 1961

The head coach for Davidson was a young man named Homer Smith. He was a two-time All-East and All-Ivy League fullback at Princeton, and he had earned his first head coaching stint at Davidson. "Smith was a great coach and a great human being," said Norris.

Coach Smith swept the team up in the locker room and looked every young man in the eye. "He told us that we were going to win the game," said Norris. "He went over four new defensive formations and five new pass plays. He told us more than once that we were going to win the game." The Wildcats emerged from the locker room a different team. Remarkably, they not only took back the momentum, Davidson won 37 to 27.

Smith went on to spend 39 years coaching football. He is the author of several books, including a popular offensive playbook.

Coaches have direct impact on game outcomes—not only through their knowledge, but through their ability to empower players to declare victory and make it so.

Smith was that sort of coach. He concluded his tenure at Davidson in 1969 with the school's lone Southern Conference championship and a berth in the Tangerine Bowl.

Declaration

In this country, we have many exquisite examples of declaration. The greatest is our own Declaration of Independence. These words, first thought and written by the young man from Virginia—and then spoken and savored by countless others—were so intentional that they had the power to create a new country.

It's very easy for the veil of history to clothe the founding fathers as legendary figures. Men who were immune from doubt or error or human weakness. But it is important to remember that when he wrote the Declaration of Independence, Thomas Jefferson was 33 years old. No doubt you've read these words—but they're worth reading again. Here are the opening lines:

IN CONGRESS, JULY 4, 1776

The unanimous Declaration of the thirteen United States of America. When in the Course of human events it becomes necessary for one people to dissolve the political bands which have connected them with another and to assume among the powers of the earth, the separate and equal station to which the Laws of Nature and of Nature's God entitle them, a decent respect to the opinions of mankind requires that they should declare the causes which impel them to the separation.

We hold these truths to be self-evident, that all men are created equal, that they are endowed by their Creator with certain unalienable Rights, that among these are Life, Liberty and the pursuit of Happiness — That to secure these rights, Governments are instituted among Men, deriving their just powers from the consent of the governed, — That whenever any Form of Government becomes destructive of these ends, it is the Right of the People to alter or to abolish it, and to institute new Government, laying its foundation on such principles and organizing its powers in such form, as to them shall seem most likely to effect their Safety and Happiness. Prudence, indeed, will dictate that Governments long established should not be changed for light and transient causes; and accordingly all experience hath shown that mankind are more disposed to suffer, while evils are sufferable than to right themselves by abolishing the forms to which they are accustomed.

Speaking from Intention

1. Denial: I am intentional when I need to be, but I can't be that way all the time.		
1	2 3 4 5	6 7 8
I can be intentional when I need to.	I know there are many times I speak too soon.	In daily conversation, I can learn to pause and *Say Something Real.*

2. Excuses: I don't have time to watch every little thing I say.		
1	2 3 4 5	6 7 8
I'm already doing everything I can.	I could do this better if I worked with like-minded people.	Some of the best outcomes will stay out of reach without Intentional Speaking.

3. Missing it: I'm not sure I can have authority without a job title.		
1	2 3 4 5	6 7 8
I'll be natural once I have authority.	I believe natural authority works for some people who are very confident in themselves.	Natural authority comes from belief in myself.

4. The gap: When someone insults me, there's no reason to wait for the gap.		
1	2 3 4 5	6 7 8
You can't let people take advantage of you.	It's always wiser to think before you speak.	Great things happen when I choose my words.

5. Doubt: It sounds good, but you don't have my job.		
1	2 3 4 5	6 7 8
How can I do this if my manager is always flying off the hook?	I might work on this with my family.	If I don't learn to be intentional at work, I will miss my part of my greatest success.

Inauthentic Speaking 5-15
Fear still holds you back 16-25
Authentic Speaking 26-40

RELEASE 3
SPEAKING FROM THE HEART

It is not only your thoughts, but your feelings,
fears and hopes that make you powerful.

Recently I sat in the back of a small auditorium, listening to a client make a budget presentation. She was dealing in numbers for the first ten minutes when suddenly she stopped. She walked away from the spread sheet, toward her listeners. Her voice became more conversational and she told a personal story. I watched the energy of the entire room go from slouching to leaning forward.

We imagine speaking from the heart is about getting emotional and sugar-coated. But speaking from the heart takes guts, because the heart knows what the brain can't figure out with all its reasoning.

> Do you want to be a
> power in the world?
> Then be yourself.
>
> – Ralph Waldo Emerson

"Grace" Edited
Bill Simmons

I met Bill Simmons on Valentine's Day in 2006. He participated in one of my workshops. When the session was over, we were having coffee when I asked if he planned to do anything special for Valentine's Day. He said it was enough for him to celebrate his 37th anniversary of surviving Vietnam. He told me this story.

On Valentine's Day in 1970, he was all of 21 years old. He was an Army infantry sergeant in the western part of Vietnam. He and his men were walking through a big wooded area. He had taken the lead when he saw a trip wire across a pathway. He told his men to circle up for an ambush and cut the wire.

The North Vietnamese Army came upon them. During the fire fight that ensued, Bill was on one side of a huge log, and one of his men was on the other. The young man was panicking and having trouble with his M16. Bill was telling him to slow down and breathe. Just at that moment, a grenade came in and landed right beside Bill. He dove over the log, but in what seemed like a long space in time, the grenade didn't go off. It just didn't go off. The events of that day would earn him the Purple Heart, but his memory is always tuned to that space in time.

Bill reflected for a moment and shook his head. "It's hard for me to explain," he said with a catch in his throat, "but it was God's grace. I knew it then, and I know it now."

The business ego will tell you that it is inappropriate to tell such a story. Yet life experiences, regardless of where they take place, do not come packaged without heart. Not for a veteran who celebrates Valentine's Day, and not for a dad who loves his sons.

"Thoughts on Life" Edited
John R. Miller

John Miller is an attorney. He has two sons, John, Jr. and Joe. A sentimental smile crosses John's face when he says, "We're very close. We're friends."

Coincidentally both young men went through business school at the same time. Before they graduated, one from Virginia and one from Columbia, John wanted to give them something meaningful.

"I decided to write down my thoughts on life," says John. And so, over the months leading up to their graduations, he wrote wherever he could—on airplanes and in waiting rooms. On scraps of paper, he recorded his philosophy and lessons learned. He couldn't very well give them the scraps, so he found an on-line source for publishing on demand and had the scraps organized by subject, ranging from the trivial to what he called "matters of great weight."

John named the book *Mere Dictum*. It covered his thoughts on everything from beer and bourbon, to religion, God, leadership, duty and honor. He gave it to each of his sons at their graduations and they were moved. Upon reading it, Joe called from Alaska to thank his dad.

Having the confidence that you will give a perfect presentation is useless. Real confidence is knowing you will misspeak, struggle for the right word, forget where you were and make mistakes—and that you can easily recover from these things when you are speaking from the heart. This is confidence.

"I came to realize," says John, "that sharing my thoughts about life with my sons was not really a gift to them, but to me." "I am not a philosopher, nor am I a writer," he said, "but I think I am...a half decent dad."

The Heart of a Leader

We are starved for genuine communication—and we all love that rare moment when someone breaks through the noise and says something deeper. Everyone knows something real has happened. It gives other people permission to speak from the truth of their own experience. Full self-acceptance can be infectious. Why is this so difficult to understand in business?

For the past century or so, we've promoted super-achievers from sales into leadership roles. These solo-performers are indispensable rain-makers but poorly typecast as leaders.

Today our definition of leadership is in flux since we realize a true leader is not your average bear. A true leader loves mining for potential in employees. A leader has the drive to speak from the heart and empower others.

What exactly does it mean to speak from the heart? The heart represents more than love and emotion. It represents the pulse that keeps us going. It represents our quest for meaning. It represents the spirit and wisdom employees are seeking today.

So often, when we make a business presentation or speak to a group, we try to be perfect. We stay on script. We focus on the words. We use expert terms. This is exhausting. Perfection is not human— in fact, it's kind of creepy.

What we want when we hear you speak is *you*—the person we can't get anywhere else, which includes the flaws. Can you speak to us without the safety of notes? Can you talk to us about things that matter to you and let your humanity show? Can you share a personal story?

Authentic leaders have the best interests of the company and its employees at heart. They understand that to assert great vision beyond the status quo, we must have the knowledge *and* speak from the heart.

> *This above all: to thine own self be true,*
> *And it must follow, as the night the day,*
> *Thou canst not then be false to any man.*
> Hamlet Act 1, scene 3, 78–82

Speaking from the Heart

1. Fear of appearing emotional: I don't talk about things that matter to me at work.

1	2 3 4 5	6 7 8
Emotion is a sign of weakness in my business.	I can speak from the heart if I am with a small group of people I know well.	Transparency is a rare and bold way of being.

2. Fear of losing control: I want to be in control when I speak.

1	2 3 4 5	6 7 8
I don't want to apologize for my emotions.	It's alright to show people you care, but you have to keep it together.	If I am tied up controlling myself I can't connect with listeners.

3. Fear of risk: Everyone expects me to use slides and a flowchart. They might think I'm crazy if I start telling stories.

1	2 3 4 5	6 7 8
People really just want the facts.	I want to be conversational but I am careful to stick with the hard content.	Risk is a great opportunity.

4. Business isn't personal: Ultimately business people have to make money.

1	2 3 4 5	6 7 8
Business is business.	Unfortunately, this is the way of the world.	The best business people don't distinguish between personal and work behavior.

5. It too cliché: I don't even like the term, "speaking from the heart."

1	2 3 4 5	6 7 8
It sounds sugar-coated.	Once in a while it is the right thing to do.	It takes guts to speak not only from the head but the heart.

Inauthentic Speaking 5-15
Fear still holds you back 16-25
Authentic Speaking 26-40

RELEASE 4
SPEAKING FROM ORIGINAL THOUGHT

You are the only source of what is not already out there in great supply.

In the spring of 1990 I went on retreat in the Blue Ridge Mountains of North Carolina. After 12 years of struggling with anxiety and alcohol, I was sober. I stayed in an old lodge, overlooking Black Mountain. The view was stunning.

There was a large makeshift book store on the main level of the lodge. There were tables and tables of books on philosophy, religion, community—and a few on writing. I picked up a used paperback book entitled *If You Want to Write: A Book about Art, Independence and Spirit*, by Brenda Ueland, first published in 1938.

> We must try to find our True Conscience, our True Self, the very Center, for this is the only first-rate choice-making center. Here lies all originality, talent, honor, truthfulness and courage.
>
> – *Brenda Ueland*

I put the book under my arm and went to the porch. I flopped down in a giant rocker and devoured that book. Ueland's central idea was that everyone is original and has something of vital importance to say.

Brenda Ueland became something of a drawstring for my past and my future. I have always loved the communications business—and business people. Today my passion is to help business people speak to one another in an authentic way.

I work with amazing one-of-a-kind people. In the beginning of their careers they all seem to have had mentors they admired and imitated. But eventually, we all have to speak from original thought to have a great career and life.

Your Own Material

Billy Crystal tells a story about the advice he received as a young comedian in 1974. He was performing at Catch a Rising Star in New York. Jack Rollins, one of the top managers in the business, was in the audience. Billy did his imitations of Muhammad Ali, Howard Cosell and Mr. Rogers, and the crowd loved him.

Don't tell other people's stories. You are not in those stories. But you were there when your child was born; you were there when your granddad died, you were there when you got your first break. Tell us your stories.

Billy was thinking that he was probably impressing Jack Rollins. But afterward Jack told him that while his imitations were great, there wasn't one inch of the real Bill Crystal in that show. He went on to say that Billy would never be memorable as long as he avoided taking the risk of saying something real.

Billy took the advice to heart. Of course he has achieved amazing success. When you use your own material—your own stories—you do your own stuff. There is nothing that comes close to your own experience.

Original Character

"Kal" Kardous is a local celebrity and an exquisitely original character. He has a trademark accent, which he used as a spokesperson for his office equipment company for 20 years before selling his business in 2008.

His charm comes from his spontaneous storytelling. He has no filter between his mind and heart and his mouth. He will say anything.

Kal came to the United States from Damascus, Syria, to attend college at the University of Wisconsin in 1969. After school, and quite by accident, he got a job selling photocopiers in Chicago. He went door-to-door carrying one of those early model portable machines.

After researching several cities that had the right economic climate to start a business, Kal moved to Charlotte in 1971. From there he became the largest independent dealer of office equipment in the region. He built that success on a combination of business savvy, humor and civic networking.

"Tell People Who You Are" Unedited
Kal Kardous

"I remember my first day on the job going door to door. Ah, that was tough. My first knock was so soft that nobody heard. I have this accent, you know, and I was afraid no one would understand what I was saying. Finally a nice lady let me show her a copier. She wanted her boss to see the copier the next day.

I went back to meet her boss, a very successful Jewish lawyer. His wall was covered with things that showed his pride in Israel. He said, 'Where are you from, India?' I nodded, afraid to say I was born in Syria…I thought he would send me away.

Later my boss had me go back to ask for referrals. I walked into his office and he said, 'What part of India are you from?' I stopped for a second and I said, 'I was born in Syria.' He said, 'Its okay. Sit down.'

He did not send me away. This man asked me about the kind of life I had growing up in Syria; I asked him about Israel. Before you knew it, we were friends. He was one my greatest supporters. He gave me leads and referrals and he helped me be successful.

I learned to tell people who you are. A man will or won't accept you. But if you lie about who you are, he will never be your friend.

If you lie about who you are—by going with the status quo and omitting your most original thoughts—we will never know you. And who you are is infinitely more interesting than the status quo."

"Real Cowboy" Edited
Bill Toole

Bill Toole is a litigator. People who know Bill say he is a storyteller who is at home in the courtroom. He will tell you that life itself is a string of stories.

In one of our sessions, Bill was asked to speak about living legends. After reflecting, Bill told us about a real cowboy named Ray Hobby.

Bill met Ray one summer when he worked on a horse farm in Silva, North Carolina. Ray was 24 at the time. He drove a pickup and kept a lariat in the back behind the bench seat. He hadn't seen a job he couldn't do with that lariat.

One day the owner of the horse farm asked him if he could trim a tree. Ray had never trimmed a tree. But he took that lariat, shinnied up the tree, and trimmed the top.

Bill had another friend on the horse farm—a short fellow named Taylor Dunn. When Ray met Taylor he told him he would be great for the "Buddy Pickup."

Bill explained that the Buddy Pickup is when you run by a fellow and swing him up on the back of your horse. The idea is that you're saving a buddy from a stampede. They decided to try it, but Ray picked up Taylor and swung him so hard he missed the rump of the horse and slammed him up against the fence—knocking Taylor out.

> The people we always love and admire most are the ones who were completely and utterly themselves

Taylor went on to become a songwriter for Reba McIntyre; he even wrote a song about Ray.

"The first thing you noticed about Ray was that his face was scarred from a house fire when he was a young boy," said Bill. "But his personality was so strong that he always had the best dates. I'll never forget that about Ray. He could do anything. He was one of the more remarkable men that I've ever met."

Speaking from Original Thought

1. Missing it: I'm not ready to go willy-nilly and say whatever pops in my head.		
1	2 3 4 5	6 7 8
Original thoughts can be inappropriate.	I have some good ideas but I am not always confident about voicing them.	Every person at the table contributes an important and unique perspective.

2. Fear of risk: My boss is not interested in hearing my original thoughts.		
1	2 3 4 5	6 7 8
My boss just wants the job done.	You have to have a sense of timing before you offer up an idea or a unique approach.	My goal is to show up as myself in every conversation.

3. Fear of being rejected: People will think I'm crazy.		
1	2 3 4 5	6 7 8
I don't want to clash with anyone.	If I can develop a relationship first, then I can share my insights.	It's a waste of time to hold back on who you are.

4. Imitation: I read the room and go with the winners.		
1	2 3 4 5	6 7 8
When I can tell how the room is leaning, I go along.	I still have room to do original work.	My goal is to be fully released into my own authenticity.

5. Image management: I "manage" my image within the company by being politically correct.		
1	2 3 4 5	6 7 8
Who doesn't?	I believe in being yourself, but I'm not an idiot.	I believe the ultimate freedom is transparency.

Inauthentic Speaking 5-15
Fear still holds you back 16-25
Authentic Speaking 26-40

SECTION III

SEVEN PRACTICES OF AUTHENTIC SPEAKING

We are not after technique—we are after your awareness. And you must practice awareness, not technique. The danger of learning technique without letting go is that technique does not carry the heat of real expression. Technique does not carry humility, intention, heart and originality.

If there is one thing you should take away from this book it is this: the world doesn't need you to fit into anything but your own skin. What we need today is not only your deep knowledge, but your experience, insights and stories of what life has taught you.

We need your leadership—which is not an exact or impersonal science. You use what you have. And for many people, authenticity is the discovery that what they have is more than enough. First, begin noticing how you show up.

7 Practices of Authentic Speaking

1 Show Up
2 Learn and Let Go
3 Focus Outward
4 Allow Silence
5 Speak Story
6 Design Simplicity
7 Take Leaps

PRACTICE 1
SHOW UP

Stop, Focus, Connect and Listen

Recently a large troupe of improv artists pulled off a stunt at Grand Central Station. Over 200 people were scattered across the main concourse, bustling like busy New Yorkers when, at the exact same time, they became frozen like mannequins. For the duration of the five-minute stunt, commuters stopped in their tracks and became mesmerized by this suspension of time.

When things stop, we notice. When there's a gap in the noise, we pay attention. When you step up to the front of a room, you have an opportunity to stop. There's no difference between the start of a meeting or the beginning of a presentation. Both are conversations. And each beginning is the crucial moment. This is the time to take a breath, and look people in the eye.

But what is our instinct? We launch right in to talking without really seeing who's in the room—without connecting. We run our mouths, non-stop, through the entire presentation. Yet it is the fearless, intentional pause that captures our attention.

Focus

As a communicator, the most important muscle you have is the one that allows focus. For years I rushed through meetings and presentations while listening to my own concerns. I was constantly wondering what I should cover and how I was doing.

Someone suggested that I read *The Inner Game of Tennis* by Tim Gallwey. And while there was nothing in his book about meetings or presentations, his wisdom applies: practice bringing your mind back to the meeting gently; tune into the present; don't over-try, just practice; develop relaxed concentration.

Connect

Eye contact is a form of silent communication that has no rival. But many of us have fallen into the habit of diverting our eyes as though we are always on a crowded sidewalk.

> **If you talk to everybody, you talk to nobody, but if you talk to one person, you talk to everybody.**
>
> – *Ronald Reagan*

Small children hang over a parent's shoulder and watch us with wide-eyed, unflappable amazement, as though we are a new species. We stare back in the same spirit. As we age, our brain creates an inner world of multi-level thought. In our careers we are subjected to Sophisticated Bull. We trust less and we spend more time within than without. We close ourselves off from strangers.

We could all stand to recapture innocence when we look people in the eye. Because this innocence is catching, and people will return it in kind. Like small children, we shouldn't over-think expressions on the faces of listeners. Don't look away when your eyes touch upon a frown. Chances are they are not frowning at you.

The proverb, "The eyes are the windows to the soul," has been with us so long it's origins are shrouded in mystery. The Reverend Billy Graham is known for his penetrating, pale blue eyes that literally seem to cast a light. Good listeners are able to hold a listening space for you with their eyes. Mothers can quiet their children across the room—with their eyes.

Most people assume they have pretty good eye contact, but they actually look around the room like a pin ball, bouncing off one person to the next. Or they sweep the room from side to side—attempting to see everybody at one time.

When you stop and hold the gaze of one person at a time for just seconds, you create a personal closeness that makes people want to stop and pay attention. It takes practice to turn around bad habits. Begin by noticing how you make eye contact throughout the day—at work or at the grocery. Do you really look people in the eye?

In 1994 I saw Paul McCartney perform at a large amphitheater. It was a soft summer night and his music rolled out over the crowd like a blanket. McCartney's voice has been something of a constant in my life. That night he played soulfully, holding the audience with his eyes. The intimacy of his communication made me feel as though he was looking right at me.

You can shorten the distance between you and listeners with your eyes. If you are speaking to a large group, you connect by transmitting the spirit of intimacy with your eyes. Connect with the listeners in the forward part of the room, and then project the connection by "looking into the eyes" of listeners in the back of the room.

Listen

Trust yourself to stop and listen. Instead of pushing to dominate a conversation, find places to stop and let other people respond. Observe where the interest is going. This is how you have dialogue. When you relax and offer a collaborative conversation to people, they know it immediately. Together you create a rich medium of communication.

You also "listen" by knowing who you're talking to. Let people know you value their time, their opinions and their perspectives. Find out as much as you can about them. You will get much more done.

> Eighty-five percent of success in life is showing up.
>
> – Woody Allen

There are many moments worth stopping for in life. It's easier to glance at the person before averting our eyes and moving by. To engage, we have to stop. We have to look and listen—and invest a moment of our time. When we delude ourselves by thinking that we don't have time to do this, we are missing everything.

PRACTICE 2
LEARN AND LET GO

Learn your instrument, then forget all that shit and wail. – Charlie Parker

There are a ton of "how-to" books out there about effective communication. My clients tell me about tricks and tips, shortcuts and secrets. Techniques can become junk food for your inner critic. So instead of being in the moment, a part of you is worried about not doing it right. And no matter how good the technique may be, the people who you are talking to can tell when you're not there.

This chapter offers the theme: Notice, Practice. The best way to learn your own instrument of expression—the human body—is through relaxed learning.

Imprisoned

When Michelangelo wrote about his sculpture, he said he could see an angel within the block of marble. He would then work to free the figure imprisoned in the marble. What a marvelous metaphor. Not finishing a sculpture, not bringing the work to life, but racing to liberate the one inside.

Who has not felt like an incomplete piece of art? Especially at work? We know we've got an original way of showing up—we know there's a real somebody inside there—but because of the pressure of expectations and our own self-consciousness, we stay trapped in the bedrock of who we think we ought to be.

Many of us think that business presentations are a medium of non-movement, except the movement done by our mouths. We act as if the real message is buried in the content of our slides.

But within you there is an authentic communicator: it's you leaning forward as you confide in your sister at the kitchen table; belly laughing with your best friend; cheering when your child hits a home run; tearing up during *Old Yeller*. And it's you making a stand. It's a force, and you can release it into your work.

Natural Vocal Color

Uncompromised vocal expression is easiest to see in young children. Before the properness of adulthood, children are free to dance, sing, shriek and giggle. Their voices aren't supposed to sound any particular way; they are simply wonderful instruments to be discovered.

But what happens? After being socialized, schooled, paid and promoted, we develop serious business voices and Sophisticated Bull. We give monotone presentations and we run robotic meetings.

Anyone who has ever spoken on the radio knows that the radio will subdue the color in your voice, so you have to crank it up a little to break through. In the same way, the work place will dampen our voices if we let it. We have to stretch over the threat of going flat.

> Children laugh an average of 146 times a day; adults laugh an average of 4 times a day.

"It's not what you said..."

We all know the rest of the line: "It's the way you said it."

In *Blink*, Malcolm Gladwell describes a study in which researchers recorded conversations between physicians and their patients. Roughly half of the physicians in the study had never been sued. The other half had been sued at least twice.

The surgeons who had never been sued used a warm, concerned tone of voice. They were also more likely to take their time and engage the patient, asking, "Can you tell me more about that?" Surgeons in the sued group tended to spend less time and use a dominant tone of voice. The difference was in how they talked to their patients and for how long, not in the quality of diagnosis given.

When we first meet you, we pick up friendliness or aggression on a primal level. An unfriendly or domineering tone of voice, subconscious or not, is a red flag. Even if you never give another business presentation in your life, you should be aware that your tone of voice is a powerful language.

Notice	Notice how you make statements such as, "I'm really excited to be here." Are you believable? Would you say it the same way to your kids? Your best teachers are your children. Listen to their bursts of spontaneity and expression.
Practice	Don't try too hard. Just come out from behind yourself in conversations and let us enjoy some real color. Play back an important voice mail before leaving it. Is it really you? Are you believable? If not, re-record it. People get fatigued listening to rambling, boring voice mails.

Face it

During the Beijing Olympic Games, when Michael Phelps smiled up from the pool, he was communicating to his mom, teammates, spectators and officials. He said something primal with his facial expression, and he said it to the people who understood his message the most. The smile is actually a form of embracing others, according to researchers like Paul Ekman.

Was this the face that launch'd a thousand ships?

– Christopher Marlow, from Doctor Faustus

Your facial expression matters—because of the instinctual assessment we conduct of one another. An unfriendly face pulls up a barrier for listeners.

Albert Mehrabian, UCLA Professor Emeritus of Psychology, studied the impact of non-verbal communication as it relates to perceived sincerity. In 1971 he released a groundbreaking study that found the way we determine if you mean what you say is 7% words, 38% vocal tone and color, and 55% visual.

This does not mean that words are not important. Mehrabian was not looking at the integrity of a lecture given to an audience of specialists. Clearly, if you are called to lecture on quantum physics, you better know your subatomic particles.

Mehrabian wanted to know how we make the decision to trust the sincerity of an individual. You say you are passionate about the organization's mission? We trust that's true by noticing if you appear to really mean what you say.

Smile for the Camera

How often, when on vacation or attending reunions, do we force ourselves to smile for the camera, rather than live in the moment?

Last year I went to a friend's wedding. The service was short, but the photos took forever. Time and time again the bride and groom smiled for the camera. After a half hour, the entire wedding party was exhausted. But they pushed on in honor of the sacred photo album, holding poses and flashing smiles.

Guillaume Duchene du Boulogne would have known if members of the wedding party were faking those smiles. A pioneer neurophysiologist back in the 1860's, he used electrical stimulation to distinguish between the genuine smile that turns up at the corners and produces little smile lines at the eyes, and the toothy smile that is produced for the camera.

> I hear and I forget
> I see and I remember
> I do and I understand
>
> – Chinese Proverb

Frequently a client tells us, "This is a serious topic—it wouldn't make sense to smile." This is not about smiling for the camera. It is about uncovering your true smile. A eulogy can be given with a reflective smile. A sad goodbye can be said with a loving smile. Authentic smiles come in different shapes and sizes—from broad to barely there.

The first time I saw myself giving a business presentation on videotape, I looked so solemn. No matter how much we tell ourselves we're being professional, there is nothing attractive about a frozen face.

Notice Notice how you carry your face throughout the day— and in meetings. Is your brow furrowed? Is your face frozen? In those moments, relax your face.

Practice Do not try too hard. Just relax your face. Smile gently at yourself, you old sourpuss. As often as possible, tell a child a fairytale. In the presence of a child, you have complete license to go into character with lots of facial expressions.

Restless Run-off

I just attended a seminar where the facilitator took her glasses off, only to put them back on. In between she held them in one hand while gesturing. She did this over and over, again and again. Like everyone else, I lost my connection to her as I anticipated the next off/on move.

Fidgeting is unnatural and distracting. When you notice yourself making repetitive movements, bring yourself gently into the moment and take a couple of purposeful steps toward a listener. You can reach for your water with a sureness of choice. Intentional movement counteracts unintentional fidgeting.

Making the choice to be still is powerful. Think about a runner at the starting line; a race horse at the gate; a diver poised on her toes.

Johnny Cash was a powerhouse. At 6'2" he seemed to fill up the whole room. When I lived in Nashville I was backstage at the Grand Ole Opry many times. One night, I looked into the Green Room and saw the "Man in Black." Since then I've often pictured Cash standing there, and realized that his presence was the way he was simply in the room without having to move. He commanded the room with physical confidence. Standing still, he had a pull that made people lean toward him.

Intentional movement—or intentional stillness poised for movement—is magnetic. Aimless shifting, unintentional fidgeting and random stepping have no pull at all. Neither does being trapped by rock.

Notice   Notice how you move and stop as you make your way throughout the activities of the day. Notice how you walk, gesture and move with purpose. Find an activity in which to show up without tension. Yoga, tai chi, walking.

Practice   You can practice your actual talk anywhere—in your office or on the patio—but practice not for the sake of technique, but to push your own expression through yourself while moving and stopping with intention.

Posture

Body language is a series of unconscious messages. We imprint an individual's posture before we make eye contact. And in every posture is a statement of energy.

Standing tall with shoulders back is not a technique. It generates positive energy that supports wellness and allows you to open your heart to others.

Closed postures—slouching, sagging, leaning away, self-wrapping, head hanging, tense hands, tense jaw and turning away—carry negative energy.

| **Notice** | Notice your postures throughout the day. When you notice you are folded up, crumpled and slouched, gently open back up. |
| **Practice** | Allow yourself to learn by noticing your own postures. Practice putting your shoulders back as you wash the car or walk the dog. |

Gently "Noticing and Practicing" is the natural learning process that will allow self-consciousness to drop away and release you into authenticity.

Freedom

The experience of self-consciousness is confining and painful. We rush to speak, glance about the room quickly, flatten our faces, lose our color, shift and step randomly.

The goal is not to use technique and "do it right." The goal is to show back up in your body—to release yourself into natural movement. You can do it by noticing when you are trapped, making an adjustment and practicing the release.

Consider Mick Jagger. He struts, pouts, jumps in his own hyper-spastic ballet. Nothing he does resembles any technique. He has leapt his way across the globe before sold out crowds in every major city in the world. Has made this freedom of expression his signature—and he has so much confidence it looks natural on him.

Should you be Mick Jagger? Probably not; the position is filled. But Mick can certainly teach us something about letting go of self-consciousness. As kids, we had no problem acting like clouds or tigers. We need to recapture some of that freedom and overcome the heaviness of adulthood.

Learn your instrument and then let go—and play soulfully.

PRACTICE 3
FOCUS OUTWARD
We cannot be in two places at the same time.

A good bit of human pain is the result of self-obsession. When we try to understand the world from within, we create anxiety over looking bad and not getting what we want. We become paranoid. We implode. The answer is not to struggle. The answer is to focus outward.

When I hear myself second-guessing how I am doing, I try to stop. I look to the listeners and ask them a question such as, "I'd like to have some feedback; what do you think?" Once I throw them the ball, I can easily pull myself out of my head and back into the room. Or, I throw myself back into the conversation by tapping into my own passion for the material.

> People have got to know whether or not their President is a crook. Well, I'm not a crook. I've earned everything I've got.
>
> – Richard Nixon

Someone said of Judy Garland, "She gave herself up to die a little bit, each time she sang." To abandon yourself to your own expression in this life, now that's something. Passion creates the willingness to put your heart out there for your listeners.

Passion is honest. Passion is never about melodramatic cheerleading. Depending on the message, passion shows up in different ways on different people. For example, when we are with a passionate human being who happens to be calm on the surface, but carries a deep intensity, we have no doubt that the earthquake is there. We can feel it.

Losing and Finding Passion

In 1977 I heard Al Gore speak in Nashville, Tennessee after he won a seat in the U.S. House of Representatives. At 28 he had dropped out of law school to run for the seat that at one time was his father's. He spoke from the heart and we loved him.

In 2000, Gore edged out the popular vote during his presidential campaign against George W. Bush. But he had so many geeky moments, those of us who knew he was brilliant were shaken. I didn't see the confidence and resolve I had seen all those years ago in Nashville.

In *Politics Lost*, Joe Klein writes that one of the reasons that Gore seemed so uncomfortable was that all his advisors fought to keep him from discussing the public policy challenges he wanted to put out there.

Today Gore has been validated with an Oscar, a Grammy, an Emmy and a Nobel Prize—not to mention enormous respect. Why? He put himself into the transmission of a message that means everything to him. He took back his passion.

Courage

You do not get power from your listeners without first giving them yours. Once you step forward in courage and offer them transparency, they will return in kind, but not before. Your listeners will begin to conspire with you to produce a great moment in communication, to create new meaning, when you offer your humanity.

Once people can see your spirit, they begin to trust you. If you are transparent, without airs or need for concealment, people will be the same way with you.

1968

One of the world's most compelling speeches was the one Robert F. Kennedy, Jr. gave on the night Martin Luther King, Jr. was assassinated.

Transport yourself back to 1968. The news of King's assassination was like a hot match, igniting riots in more than one hundred cities across the nation. Kennedy had been scheduled to appear before an inner city crowd in Indianapolis that night, and was urged to cancel. Instead he chose to have a genuine conversation with the crowd that brought a sense of peace to the city.

Ladies and Gentlemen,

I'm only going to talk to you just for a minute or so this evening, because I have some very sad news for all of you. Could you lower those signs, please? I have some very sad news for all of you, and, I think, sad news for all of our fellow citizens, and people who love peace all over the world; and that is that Martin Luther King was shot and was killed tonight in Memphis, Tennessee.

Martin Luther King dedicated his life to love and to justice between fellow human beings. He died in the cause of that effort. In this difficult day, in this difficult time for the United States, it's perhaps well to ask what kind of a nation we are and what direction we want to move in. For those of you who are black—considering the evidence evidently is that there were white people who were responsible—you can be filled with bitterness, and with hatred, and a desire for revenge.

We can move in that direction as a country, in greater polarization—black people amongst blacks, and white amongst whites, filled with hatred toward one another. Or we can make an effort, as Martin Luther King did, to understand, and to comprehend, and replace that violence, that stain of bloodshed that has spread across our land, with an effort to understand, compassion, and love.

For those of you who are black and are tempted to fill with hatred and mistrust of the injustice of such an act, against all white people, I would only say that I can also feel in my own heart the same kind of feeling. I had a member of my family killed, but he was killed by a white man.

But we have to make an effort in the United States. We have to make an effort to understand, to get beyond, or go beyond these rather difficult times. My favorite poet was Aeschylus. And he once wrote: "Even in our sleep, pain which cannot forget falls drop by drop upon the heart, until, in our own despair, against our will, comes wisdom through the awful grace of God."

What we need in the United States is not division; what we need in the United States is not hatred; what we need in the United States is not violence and lawlessness, but is love, and wisdom, and compassion toward one another, and a feeling of justice toward those who still suffer within our country, whether they be white or whether they be black.
—Robert F. Kennedy

When we speak about what is really important, our blood quickens. Passion is the energy that makes things go. It is the electricity that drives the physical body; it quite literally plugs you in and lights you up. Without it, you are simply passing along information. One of the many ways to access what is meaningful is to tell us about your mentor.

"Peter Gilchrist" Edited
Shirley L. Fulton

Shirley Fulton is one of the most well-known people in the Mecklenburg County Courthouse, having spent over 20 years as Senior Resident Superior Court Judge, Resident Superior Court Judge, District Court Judge and Assistant District Attorney.

When she graduated from Duke University School of Law, she went to work for a small firm there in Durham. The hours were long, and soon she realized she needed to devote more time to being a mother. Her son was seven and ball games were becoming very important.

One of her professors told her the District Attorney in Charlotte was looking for a prosecutor, and she arranged for Shirley to go and interview with him. On the way to Charlotte, Shirley thought, "If I become a prosecutor, I will be prosecuting people who look like me."

Shirley interviewed with Peter Gilchrist and he offered her the job. Before she left his office that day he asked, "Where do you see yourself ten years from now?" She thought, "I'm just trying to make it through the next day and get food on the table." But she didn't say that. She said, "I would like to be a judge." He said, "We'll make it happen."

Shirley worked for Peter in the District Attorney's office for more than four years, learning how the justice system worked. He encouraged and supported the members of his staff, without politics. "If you did the right thing for the right reasons, and you were called on the carpet by a victim who was unhappy," says Shirley, "you looked around and Peter was at your shoulder."

When she was approached about a District Court level position, she told Peter she was going for it, and she did. She was appointed in 1986 under Governor Jim Martin. Two years later a seat became open for a Superior Court position. She ran a statewide campaign and was unopposed. Eight years later she was re-elected while she was undergoing chemotherapy for cancer.

Shirley has overcome many life challenges to build an amazing career. "Peter Gilchrist is largely responsible for my success," says Shirley, "because of the way he treated me, and the way he ran that office."

When she retired, Peter organized a retirement party and the funding to have a portrait of her done for the Mecklenburg County Courthouse. Shirley is grateful to many people, but especially to Peter Gilchrist. She smiles broadly when she says, "I've never told him, but to my friends I refer to Peter as my Great White Father."

PRACTICE 4
ALLOW SILENCE

Silence holds enough power to say everything,
if you allow it to. This is not easy. Silence requires the
unthinkable—to do nothing, to just be in the moment.

When I was 12, I spent an amazing summer riding horses at the Nutcracker, a ranch nestled against a lake just outside Sebring, Florida. Every morning my mother dropped me off at the barn ahead of the others. I wanted to be the first one there.

As I set foot on the alley between the stalls, I was entering my church. There was no sound but an occasional low snort from one of the horses. I breathed in the magic—a tack room smells of leather and saddle soap; the feed room, of hay, corn and oats; the stalls of hay and sawdust.

One of my jobs was to slip a bridle on the big mare, Brandy, and ride her bareback down to the lake and back. She was foundered—with inflammation around her hooves—so she walked very slowly.

The two of us took this slow ride every morning, in the cool shade of pine trees, in silence. I stroked her neck and wondered if she could feel my love for her. When we got to the lake we would stand in the shallow water of the lake. It eased the swelling. We rested there in the water, in the silence.

Brandy seemed to enjoy the ride back to the barn a bit more. We were more connected in the quiet. We were happier and lighter.

Nonstop Noise

We don't allow much room in our lives to practice silence on a quiet walk or trail ride. We are all so busy we can hardly stand in line for a latte without talking. And then we talk on cell phones as we walk to and from the car. It is so noisy all of the time. And it seems like there's something we have to say every moment.

Speakers who talk nonstop actually create stress for listeners who are trying to keep up. Silence is the place in which both audience and speaker stop and focus. But pausing for a second or two of silence is a deceptively easy act. As soon as we feel the impact of adrenaline and self-consciousness, it is easier to talk.

Silence is also the place in which we connect and listen. It lets listeners know we are in that very moment with them. Ronald Reagan was admired as a communicator in part because his words were so richly paced, and he was so comfortable with silence that he drew listeners to him. What you do not say is loaded with meaning...confidence, thoughtfulness, intimacy.

| **Notice** | Notice when you've been hearing your own voice non-stop for a while. Without stressing, stop and breathe. Be content to be the one who listens in at least one conversation today. |
| **Practice** | Allow yourself to learn by taking a day, or part of a day, to practice pockets of silence. Let others complete their thoughts. Instead of rushing to speak, gently pause. |

Radiant Beams

Beethoven's 5th symphony begins with silence. The conductor raises his hand in the air and there is no sound. When it falls, the crash of the famous four notes is like thunder. Then there is another pause before those notes hit you again.

On the night of its debut in 1808, a reviewer named Hoffman called those notes "radiant beams that shoot through the deep night of this region." And, what showcases beams is the unlit space around them.

These pauses, as much as any note played on any instrument, are what make Beethoven's 5th an incomparably dramatic piece of music. The effect of a rest in music is the same as the effect of a pause in communication. Silence gives us time to understand, process, reflect and experience fully.

Meaning without Words

One of our clients is a young physician who shared with us the devastating blow he experienced in the loss of a patient. He stood in the silence, looking upward, his hands in his pockets. As the silence deepened, the meaning grew. He was not fighting the silence or pushing to find the words, he was being in the silence, with the dual force of life and death.

Meaning springs from silence. When I trust myself to pause and connect with listeners, I can capture a new relevance, and together we make a new turn. The best outcome isn't up to me—the outcome is a collaboration with the listeners.

Silence provides a place in the action where you might say something more brilliant than you could have scripted. And when we attempt to have everything buttoned-up, locked down and airtight, we abandon the possibility of our own brilliance. We also come off as sterile and inauthentic.

I kept myself stuck giving presentations this way for years, and so it was a revelation to realize I could go un-canned.

You must know your subject matter, but do not memorize. Leave room for the good stuff—to speak from the heart. If you are so committed to your own script that you cannot react well to sudden questions, interruptions or the mood of listeners, you will stumble. Yet in silence, these things are a part of the natural dialogue.

*Y*OUR PAUSES ARE AS IMPORTANT AS
THE PARTICULAR WORDS YOU USE.

———————

SILENCE IS MORE EMPHATIC THAN YELLING.

———

AND MORE POWERFUL.

———————

No kidding.

*W*HEN YOU START SLOWING DOWN,
THERE IS A PROCESS CALLED
ENTRAINMENT. THE DOMINANT
RHYTHM IS WHAT PEOPLE TAKE ON.

———————

WHISPER AND EVERYONE
WHISPERS IN THEIR HEARTS.

---

*L*EARNING TO PAUSE IS NO LESS THAN TRANSFORMATIONAL. HERE ARE SOME OF THE MANY BENEFITS OF SILENCE:

———————

A PAUSE TELLS PEOPLE, "NEW PARAGRAPH."
WE CAN'T JUST SPONGE UP THE SPOKEN
WORD WITHOUT PAUSING TO ASSIMILATE.

———————

SILENCE INVITES LISTENERS TO EXPERIENCE
THOUGHTFULNESS. IF YOU REFLECT ON
WHAT YOU'VE JUST SAID, WE WILL AS WELL.

—————————

IF YOU ARE SILENT BEFORE YOU
SPEAK, WE WILL TRUST THAT
YOUR WORDS ARE THOUGHTFUL.

———————

PAUSING WILL ELIMINATE CLUTTER. IF YOU SPEAK NON-STOP YOU WILL SURELY SAY "UM..." AND "YOU KNOW."

———————

PAUSING ALLOWS YOU TO
BREATHE. A BREATH OF AIR WILL
CALM YOU, KEEP YOUR BRAIN
FROM SHUTTING DOWN, AND
ALLOW YOUR VOICE TO PROJECT.

———————

IF YOU MAKE A CONNECTION WITH LISTENERS IN A MOMENT OF SILENCE, YOU HAVE SHARED INTIMACY.

———————

THE WILLINGNESS TO BE SILENT LETS US
KNOW YOU ARE INVITING DIALOGUE.

———————

IN THE SILENCE YOU CAN BE SPONTANEOUS.
YOU CAN PUT YOUR PERCEPTIONS INTO WORDS
AS THEY COME TO YOU. YOU CAN TAP INTO
THE POWER OF THE PRESENT MOMENT.

———

*I*N QUIET PLACES, REASON
ABOUNDS.

— *ADLAI STEVENSON*

PRACTICE 5
S<small>PEAK</small> S<small>TORY</small>

We make sense of our lives through stories.

S uppose I make these observations. We make polarized demands of business leaders; employees expect leaders to relate well and inspire trust, but stockholders expect CEOs to rule from their position and drive stock value at any cost—Or, what if I were to first tell you this story about former Wachovia CEO Ken Thompson?

"Fortune and Failure" Edited
Roger Pearce

In 1990, Roger Pearce was a commercial banker in Jacksonville, Florida. One of his biggest clients was a retailer who was being hit by the downturn of the economy. He was good friends with the CFO and spoke to him weekly. Sales were slipping, but they had high hopes for the holiday season.

"When their January financial statement was delayed, the CFO explained that the auditors had slowed things down. It was understandable," says Pearce, "but when I showed up that Friday, the CFO told me they had filed for bankruptcy an hour before."

As he drove back to the office, Pearce was gripped with anxiety. The $20 million line of credit was fully drawn. There had been unusual activity in the account. He began the unpleasant task of letting people know what was happening.

"On Monday everybody wanted to know how this had happened," says Pearce. "The meeting to discuss it started at 5:00 p.m. And nothing good ever comes of meetings that start at 5:00 p.m. Credit officers had flown down to Jacksonville to be part of this meeting and among them, Ken Thompson. The questions flew at me. At that time in my career I was just a young guy still trying to make a name for myself. After about two hours of answering as truthfully as I could, there weren't very many good answers. It happened because these things happen. It happened because in the rush of the day, I had done the best that I could, but I had missed some clues, some things I should have seen. At the end of the day I trusted too much.

> I went back to my office that day in January. It was 7:00 p.m. and it was dark. I don't know when I've felt so bad in the workplace. I put my head in my hands and cried.
>
> About that time, Ken Thompson walked in my office. He sat down and told me a story about another young banker who had missed the signals. He hadn't gotten everyone involved the way he should have. There had been a big loss. He talked to me for 45 minutes. And then he told me that he was that young banker. 'You're a good man,' he told me. 'Things work out.'
>
> I went home and I felt so much better. As I got into bed, the phone rang and it was Ken. He just wanted to make sure I was okay."

Things did work out. The bank actually recovered most of the $20 million over the next two years.

Pearce says what he learned from Ken Thompson was about leadership. Leaders lead by reaching out to their people, relating with them and sharing their own experiences.

Eighteen years later Ken Thompson faced a difficult situation of his own: a mob of angry shareholders. They wanted his head—and they got it. Thompson was officially ousted in June after a $708 million first-quarter loss.

And who can blame the stockholders? This staggering loss eventually forced America's fourth largest bank into near bankruptcy before a merger with Wells Fargo.

Even so, Thompson was loved by his employees and the people of Charlotte, North Carolina. He did not rule by position. He believed in investing in people, and you can actually feel this core value in the Wachovia culture. Roger Pearce is one of the scores of people who have history with Ken Thompson and his generosity.

Now it is much more relevant and meaningful to tell you that we rarely talk about the banishment of a CEO who was a great leader respected by employees, but all too imperfect. And there you have the power of a story.

If we researched the human ability to tell stories, we would have to look at the evolution of language. Some might say that the stories of past millennia are very different from our two stories about Ken Thompson. But no one can deny that storytelling is in our DNA.

The power of story is harnessed by everyone. Authors, advertising agencies, movie producers, lyricists, speakers and parents use story to communicate ideas that are too big to be conveyed in mere data. We are clearly story creatures. And this means that we don't have to work hard to rediscover the language of story. In many ways, we just have to stop making it so complicated. Good storytelling is a well-constructed series of powerful moments and images.

Your Stories in Business

To say you don't like "talking about yourself" is to be stingy with yourself. To say you can't tell personal stories in business is to perpetuate Sophisticated Bull. People interested in meaningful leadership are candid about their struggles and their triumphs.

Simple Formula

At the core, stories have a very simple equation: this is what happened; this is how I felt; and this is the point I care about.

1. What Happened

Simple brevity allows stories to land one punch to the imagination instead of a series of little touches. Short stories that last one to two minutes will be consumed in their entirety by the greatest number of people.

Ernest Hemingway was the master of the short sentence with long meaning. Here is the story, written in response to a challenge to tell an entire story in only six words: "For Sale: baby shoes, never used."

Hemingway's six words might be an extreme, but stories do not require length. Imagine what you can say in a minute or two:

"Baseball Card" Unedited
Mark W. Merritt

"I have a 1966 baseball card that has Mickey Mantle on it. It's a collector's item. It may look like a baseball card to you. To me, it's a bridge to a shared past. It was given to me by my brother Craig who is 22 months older than I am.

When we grew up, we were inseparable. We played baseball together—we listened to baseball games together. He would beat me up. I was the younger brother who tried to get in one good punch to make it all even. He would protect me from older kids in the neighborhood who would pick on me. I can say with a high degree of assurance that anything illegal or unlawful I ever did in my youth was the direct result of the influence of my sometimes wayward older brother.

He gave the card to me when I was 45 years old. Other people in the family thought it was crazy to give a 45-year-old a baseball card. But to me it was a reaffirmation that something we had was special and important: the shared background and shared memories. It's something no one can ever take away.

I find myself now with my older brother separated by time and distance and a professional career, and we feel disconnected. We miss each other. I can pick up this baseball card and I feel better.

Several years ago Duke University upset UNLV in a national championship game. After the game, Coach K was asked, 'How did your young group of kids beat this experienced team?' He said, 'It's because we had Grant Hill.' He said having Grant Hill on the team was like going somewhere with your older brother. He said when he went somewhere with his older brother he always felt safe, he always felt confident, he always felt protected, he always felt that he would be okay. I knew exactly what he meant.

Now, years and years after we sat up at night listening to Yankees games together, and playing baseball together, he gave this to me because he knew it would mean something to me, like nothing else could. It's probably the favorite gift I ever received."

Everyday Life

Stories do not live outside everyday life. Stories show up in self-introductions, intimate chats, high-stakes conversations, business presentations and everything in between. Story moments are everywhere and happening all the time—as you meet with clients, attend ballgames and drive the kids home from school.

Vicky Mitchener is an energetic entrepreneur who has built a unique culture of work-life balance at her real estate firm. To tell us what is important to her, Vicky told this story.

She was driving her daughter, Ruffin, and her friends home from school. With that one perfect ear that all mothers have, she overheard the conversation on the back seat. The girls were talking about their moms, who they wanted to dress like on Freaky Friday—and who was the "coolest mom."

Ruffin's best friend piped up and said, "I want to be like Mrs. Mitchener. She's got a briefcase and she's a cool mom." Vicky said, "I laughed out loud. Somehow these little girls were telling me I had all I've ever wanted—to be a good mother to my kids and a great career. I want to make this possible for the folks who work with me—both, without having to choose more of one and less of another."

2. This is What I Experienced and How I Felt

Brevity has nothing to do with vague shortcuts. Some of the ways that we distance ourselves in communication is through generalization and nameless characters.

If you tell us what you were experiencing, we will experience it with you.

Peter Buck is an attorney in Charlotte and a wonderful storyteller. Consider his story about a specific man who gave him advice, at a specific time in his life.

"Two Things" Unedited
Peter Buck

"I've had lots of advice in my life, but the advice I remember I got when I was in law school during my very first interview in the fall of my second year. I remember it vividly. I flew to New York City and had interviews with Dewey Ballantine and Sullivan Cromwell.

The Dodgers were in the World Series that night and they had Ron Cey and Davey Lopes playing, and so I was really fired up for my big interview trip. I had done better than I thought I would in my first year, and I was getting invited to these firms in New York.

I went over to Dewey Ballantine in my brown and orange plaid, double knit suit. I looked pretty good. The last interview was with the Senior Tax Partner, Bob Fullem, who has I think since passed away. He talked to me for about 10 minutes, mostly making me feel good about how good I was.

Then he told me, 'All that lawyers have to sell, Peter, is two things: brains and decency. That's what we sell here. That's what you'll need to sell wherever you are. If you come here you're going to have both.' I've taken it with me ever since. He was right. That's what we have to sell—brains and decency—to all the people we deal with. It has been the best advice I ever received."

Who could forget that young man in the brown and orange plaid suit? Not only is it memorable, we know that Peter Buck is the real deal.

When you tell us a story, consider what you were seeing, hearing, touching, tasting, smelling and feeling. We can see the car if you tell us it was a gold Cadillac. We can taste the fruit, if we can see juicy slices of pineapple. We can hear the bird, if we know it was a Mourning Dove.

3. Why I told the story

Reliving an important moment kicks up a sort of generative experience for listeners. That is to say, a story told from the heart allows the listener to create his or her meaningful moment. When you guide us into a message through story, we understand something more than just the words that you use. We find ourselves in the context of your story.

A few years ago, I heard a counselor named Tom speak on behalf of a fundraising campaign for the children's home where he worked.

Tom asked everyone to close their eyes and recall their childhood experiences of summer. He gave us images of running barefoot, playing in the sprinkler and the smell of chlorine at the pool. He described the joy of catching lightning bugs at night and lying in the cool grass to gaze up at the stars.

Then Tom asked us to imagine the life of a young boy who had just arrived at the home. One whose family had abandoned him. One who had no possessions other than an extra t-shirt. This man was giving us the big picture by evoking sensation. In a matter of minutes we all understood.

What Happened
Simple Brevity
Powerful Moment

+

How I Felt
Specifics, Sensory Images
of seeing, hearing, touching, tasting, smelling

+

Why I Told the Story
Meaningful Point

=

New Insights and Meaning for listeners

It's a crying shame that business people feel ill equipped to tell stories—and think storytelling is some sort of fairytale way of communicating. Recently a senior executive with a public utilities corporation said to me, "I don't tell stories." She went on to prove that not only could she tell stories, she had fascinating stories to tell. She came from an extraordinary family, and before her success as an executive, she spent time on the runway as a New York model.

Clients are surprised by the library of their own stories, the easy transference of meaning through metaphor, and their ability to show up in the moment with passion. In this state they can spark the minds of others and reach a new or forgotten level of meaning in communication.

"Going Back" Edited
Peter Popovich

All of us have stories from the events and key experiences that have shaped our lives. To uncover them, we'll have to look back.

Peter Popovich is a first generation immigrant from the former Yugoslavia. As a boy growing up in a lower-middle class family of Belgrade, Peter heard stories about America, the "land of opportunity." "In my young mind," says Peter, "I imagined that money was scattered about—actually on the ground—in America."

In the winter of 1961, at the age of 9, Peter embarked on a brutal month-long journey across the Atlantic with his mother and sisters. Many of the 30 passengers on the boat suffered sea sickness the entire trip, and Peter was one of them. He could barely get out of bed, but he held fast to the image of America.

Peter remembers the Statue of Liberty as the vessel came into port, but what he remembers more vividly is an elderly gentleman who was being helped off the boat. The trip had nearly killed him. As he stepped on to the ground he waved off his helpers, dropped to his knees and kissed the earth.

"There are a handful of life events so powerful," says Peter, "I can go back to and relive them in my mind and heart. The image of that old man kissing the ground is one of them. I was in America."

Sankofa

"Sankofa" (SAN-KO-FA), is a West African word meaning "go back and fetch it." It also describes the process of going back to collect the wisdom of yesterday, in order to build for the future. If you will connect with your own experiences deeply enough, your stories will resonate with everyone.

To capture story moments from the past, spark your recall by interviewing your relatives and looking at photos. Each of us has experienced turning points or defining moments along the timeline of life. If you were to identify all of your Life Events, you would have a constellation of story moments. Respond to any of these prompts that bring to mind a story moment:

- A mistake I made—and what happened
- A decision I made that changed my life for the better
- First jobs, new jobs, losing jobs
- An experience that has shaped my philosophy
- A tough obstacle I had to overcome
- Something I had to learn the hard way
- My role model for leadership—my mentor

Once you identify an event that has heat, carry it around with you and let it simmer. As images come up, jot them down. You don't have to have the whole thing right away. But if you give your story time and space, it will grow. Follow the most powerful emotions and images and you'll find your story fleshing itself out (seemingly) on its own.

> Trust me, there is nothing that makes you feel more Fully Alive than being "in the zone" (as athletes call it). Once you've been there, you never want to leave.
>
> – Tom Peters on Speaking

Bring home a story

Every day, every interaction is a story idea. Notice when you go into situations that have an interesting texture, and be curious. Ask some great questions.

A few years ago I was traveling during the holidays and found myself snowed in at the O'Hare Airport in Chicago for 24 hours. I could not believe my luck. I was cranky with the woman at the gate, who was just doing her job. I huffed and puffed until I was sick of myself—and I surrendered to the situation.

In the lounge I met a fellow traveler named Barbara who had a background in broadcasting similar to mine. I asked her opinion on a variety of things and she gave me perspectives I would have never thought of. She inspired in me new ideas and when she left I wrote in my journal for two hours.

> If you are interested in meaningful leadership, work on understanding the story of your life. Not your life's timeline, but the experiences that have shaped you.

Think of yourself as a reporter. Every time you venture out, bring home a story.

Practice, to quiet the mind

Your brain is the nemesis of Authentic Speaking. You can't stop thinking when you speak, but with practice, you can stop analyzing yourself and your message.

When we begin to consider using a personal story, the negative voice (the one afraid of looking bad) questions the validity of what we have to say.

When Fred Astaire was asked why he practiced dance steps for hours upon hours, he replied, "To dance as though I haven't practiced."

Practice telling your story, in the way you actually speak. Practice for the approval of your left brain, so you don't have to think through it when you speak.

There is a state of speaking that is called "the zone." It happens when you have immersed yourself in your story and no longer have to think about it. The message seems to roll through you and you can enjoy the ride, and you say things that are a brilliant result of being in that moment and time.

PRACTICE 6
DESIGN SIMPLICITY

Simplicity is the ultimate sophistication. —Leonardo da Vinci

All our lives we've been told to keep it simple. Why is this so hard to understand? Why is it so hard to do? Why are we constantly tempted to overload people?

Our clients tell us they dread outlining and organizing material. We don't blame them since all this sounds dreadful.

Design Simplicity is the creative approach that liberates Authentic Speaking and Presenting.

A Design for Simplicity:

a guide for creating your presentation;
a natural process of organizing and outlining.

There are five ingredients of presentation design. These ingredients are highly interconnected and not necessarily sequential steps.

1. High Concept
2. Facts and Knowledge
3. Feeling, Imagination and Story
4. Motive and Purpose
5. Scene Setter and Final Scene

1. High Concept

In the movie business, stories begin with a "High Concept." Behind all performances, special effects and even the script—there is one big idea. And when you get right down to it, a great presentation and a great movie are similar. They both require a powerful idea.

When I was earning my BA in Journalism at the University of Mississippi, I studied under Dr. Norton, a tough professor who liked to project your story on the wall and dismantle it in front of the entire class.

I had the entertainment beat for the campus newspaper. One weekend in '77, I covered the Leon Russell concert. Russell was touring with his wife, Mary, to promote *The Wedding Album.*

An hour past showtime, the band had not taken the stage. The crowd was getting drunk and irritated. Backstage, the saxophone player, Marty Grebb said, "Mary's drunk. Happens every night." Mary never went on, but Leon saved the day and kept everyone on their feet for two hours.

My article led with a favorable review of Leon and mentioned Mary halfway through the article. The next morning Dr. Norton critiqued my review by saying, "You missed it. The real story was Mary. She should have been your lead and your headline. The real story is the drug and alcohol abuse."

Before your presentation, ask yourself, "Did I get the lead right, or have I missed it?" Identify the High Concept and go where the energy is. Otherwise, you'll dance around the good stuff.

If I were going to make a presentation on this story, here's the approach I might have taken:

- High Concept: Drug and Alcohol Abuse in Pop Culture
- Facts, Knowledge and Understanding: Statistics on drug abuse and an understanding of what they mean
- Feeling, Imagination and Story: Mary, passed out backstage
- Motive and Purpose: Are college kids living in a parallel culture? Do I believe this message is valuable?
- Scene Setter and Final Scene: Intriguing Introduction and Close that honors my message

2. Facts + Knowledge

Never settle for the facts alone. You must add deep knowledge and an understanding of what the facts mean—as minimum credibility for a great presentation. But tiny details, truckloads of information and complex logic are deadly, especially when people are hearing the information for the first time.

This is not about quantity. I used to show up with too much material. As a result, I felt distracted and scattered with deciding what I had time to cover. If I decided to cover too much I would have to do a little fire-hosing. The key is to allow for enough space within the structure, where people can absorb what you are giving them. Once again here is the Content Ladder:

Level I	Stand-alone, logical facts
Level II	Knowledge and understanding of what the facts mean—and an overview of what is known in your field
Level III	Level II plus: creativity, imagery and stories to produce new relevance for listeners
Level IV	Level III plus: wisdom to value humanitarian concepts and global impact

This is not about minutia. After all, do listeners care about the provisions that were aboard the Santa Maria? For the general audience, too much material causes brain overload. Less is more.

Authentic leaders are not those who give us the most facts. They are the ones who are most informed and can put the facts together in a way that helps us understand ourselves and the world around us.

3. Feeling, Imagination and Story

I cannot imagine a presentation that would not improve with humanization. Even when you've been asked to come in and present the budget, you bring your "story" (your experience and insights) with you. We could just look at the spreadsheet ourselves if it were the only thing we wanted. What we want in addition to the numbers is your story, summary and the big picture.

The previous chapter looked at personal stories. There is also a universe of story elements that exist in quotes, word histories, movies, the newspaper, web sites and everywhere you turn.

Once we glimpse the inauthentic approach we've taken to speaking and presenting we can crack the door on a natural way of doing things. Begin with your interests. What do you love to talk about? What draws your natural curiosity?

Teddy

Consider this story about Teddy Roosevelt, who is one of the defining characters in American history. He was our 26th president, a passionate speaker and the man for whom the Teddy bear was named. He was also the force behind the Panama Canal, the Pure Food and Drug Act, the break up of corporate monopolies, and the creation of five national parks and 18 national monuments.

In October of 1912 he gave a speech to an enthusiastic crowd in Milwaukee, Wisconsin. Just before he took the stage, a man stepped out of the crowd and shot him in the chest with a .45 caliber pistol. The shooter's bullet passed through Roosevelt's front pocket, his folded script and eyeglass case—which slowed the bullet enough to save his life. Roosevelt was able to put a clean handkerchief into the superficial wound and deliver an amazing speech. The crowd went wild and another Roosevelt legend was born.

What is the crux of the story about Teddy Roosevelt? It is not about getting shot. It's about Roosevelt's resolve to go on. The idea resonates with us, because these are the kind of virtues we look for in leaders. Perseverance and courage. Every story or vignette carries the potential for being an encoded message—a metaphor.

Dig and Scan

There is a natural way of gathering material. Notice the interest you have in magazines, books and the newspaper. This idea might make you feel tired if you don't believe you have any extra time to gather anything.

When I was in broadcasting, we circulated trade magazines with a routing slip. As the trades piled up on my desk, I felt mounting pressure and guilt. When I couldn't stand it, I would pass them off to someone else on the routing slip. Everyone else was doing the same thing, so we circulated a pile of trades from office to office.

Today I am a digger-scanner-reader. I have taken myself off the hook for reading cover-to-cover. I peruse a book by flipping to the Contents, and forward to the sections that stand out. From there I scan. If I am hooked, I read the rest. It's my reader-friendly-system.

It's best not to allow the pressure to build. I try to respond to a new magazine when it arrives—I scan the contents and bookmark the articles that resonate with me. If there is only one article, I might tear it out and toss the rest of the magazine. If there are none, I toss the entire magazine.

Quotes, Expressions, Sayings

Find your way to listeners through your own interests and passion. Consider these prompts.

- Sayings you heard from your grandparents
- Great lines from films
- Blogs
- Family stories
- Quotes from your favorite authors
- Lyrics from your favorite singer
- Historical notes
- A metaphor that comes from nature

> ...you can free yourself from clouds of automatic verbiage, from "uninterestingness." When you get the hang of it, you will work at expressing yourself freely, pulled toward it in fascination.
>
> – Brenda Ueland

Whatever words or phrases you are fond of using, understanding the origins will make your communication more meaningful. For example, instead of using a tired phrase and suggesting that we "push the envelope," I could tell listeners where that phrase comes from:

The term comes from the risky occupation of World War II test pilots. An aircraft was said to have a certain envelope of performance—how far, fast and high it flew. A test pilot's job was to "push the envelope" on the aircraft and take it beyond where it was known to perform. When we push beyond limitations, we can do more than we thought possible.

4. Motive and Purpose

Discerning listeners want to know your motive upfront. Other listeners just want to know if you believe you are saying something worthwhile.

Either way, they're pretty good at spotting a speaker who is there for other reasons.

If you show up with a scantily clad sales pitch, they can smell it. If you are there to feign interest in the vulnerable consumer, you are done. If you are a self-serving spinmeister, stay home.

In the gap, just before you speak, choose to speak from the heart. Tell us why you care about your message. We will overlook many things if your passion and motive are true. Once the elements are in place, it's easy to design the first and final pieces. These pieces are critical.

5. Scene Setter and Final Scene

When you first step into the presence of listeners, you have an opportunity to invite them into a vibrant dialogue. When you leave the presence of listeners, you have an opportunity to leave them with something meaningful.

For example, if you're giving a presentation on branding, you might use a story about Jack Nicholson as a scene setter.

Jack tells a story about taking a class as a young actor at a theater in LA. The course was taught by a talented character actor named Joe Flynn. Joe gave Nicholson some great advice. He warned him that well-meaning people in the business would advise him to take voice lessons and change the nasal quality of his voice. Joe was right. Everyone Jack met urged him to change, but he remembered what Joe said and never took a lesson. Today Jack is one of the greatest character actors of our time—and his voice is a trademark.

If you give listeners something worth hearing at the beginning, they are with you. If you say something meaningful at the close, they will remember you.

There are an infinite number of interesting ways to craft a scene setter and final scene. We just have to be more creative than, "Hello, I'm very excited to be here," and, "So—that's it."

Here are some suggestions for scene setters and final scenes:

- Mini-story
- Metaphor
- Relevant quote
- Bold fact or striking statistic
- The core idea said creatively
- A look into the past
- A look into the future
- Thought-provoking question
- Sturdy and blunt statement

Choices, Choices, Choices

Don't let anyone tell you that there is one right way to outline. The right way is the way that makes sense to you, and there are many choices. Here are just a few:

Basic 3-Part	Open, Main Body, Close
Storytelling	This is What Happened, This is What I Experienced and How I Felt, This is the Point I Care About
PPF	Past, Present, Future
SOS	Situation, Options, Solution: Present the situation followed by the options and the best solution in your opinion.
Challenge, Opportunity	Present the Challenge, Offer the Solution and Opportunity
Case Study	Present the Case Study—and move to the principles demonstrated by the case study.
Assumption, Fallacy	Disprove a commonly held belief.
Compare and Contrast	Set up two scenarios that in their very contrast make a statement.
Rhetorical Question	Suppose you could not fail. What would you do?
Numeric	"Five Steps to…"
Chronology	Presentation follows a narrative timeline.
PREP	My Position, Reasons, Evidence, Position Restated
Tell Them	Tell them what you're going to tell them. Tell them. Tell them what you've told them.

Only Words?

A look at the design of a presentation is not complete without a look at words themselves. Researchers believe that the oldest spoken language is Mayan, which was around 7,000 years ago when the Maya migrated into Mexico. The first written language, Cuneiform, was recorded by the Sumerians. The single word at the beginning of all languages seems to have been "Papa." We are all connected by a single word.

Imagine. In more than 5,000 years we've progressed all the way to this:

The fact that we bring to the table the knowledge capital around industry technology necessary to build processes and flow for the large scale change resulting from this merger provides the differentiation that will ultimately provide discernable value to the customer and stockholder.

> In the beginning was the word and the word was with God and the word was God (John 1:1).

What would the Sumerians think of the job we've done, handling their miraculous seed of language?

Words are so much more than clumps of sound. Words are really the symbols we exchange to make meaning of our world. There are patterns behind the way people who are in the same organization or family use words, and researchers study these patterns to learn about how that group constructs their reality.

We can do better than speaking from the surface layer of language with business buzz words. No one is meant to speak with eloquence in everyday life, all the time. After all, we have to say, "Pass the salt" and we have to ask, "Where is your restroom?" But when it's time to communicate deeper meaning, we need to be able to drop the slang.

Good Words, Right Order

Patrick McLean is a creative consultant who is as Anti-Sophisticated-Bull as anyone I've ever met. His "Good Words Right Order" curriculum allows executives to capture what they are trying to communicate without over-thinking the process. Which is important because writing is a little like golf. The ball doesn't go anywhere—so why is it so hard to hit? You can rewrite a sentence as many times as you want. So why is it so hard for people to write well?

Patrick gives people some very simple suggestions. Sometimes the simplicity is profound, but mostly he gives them permission to forget the rules and express themselves. Because the goal of writing is not play by the rules. The goal of writing is to communicate clearly and powerfully. Sure, grammar is supposed to help, but as Patrick said, "Nobody's ever going to notice if you use the subjunctive wrong, but they'll get very frustrated if you don't make some kind of point."

Watching Patrick teach the other day I began to think about speaking and writing as natural forces that come through us. Language and words are fun when we're kids, and then we start over-thinking and generalizing everything.

The worst form of Sophisticated Bull may be the vague generalization. And it's so much easier to spot in its written form. When you don't know what you're trying to say, or you're not too sure if you should say it, it's tempting to turn to sweeping generalities and jargon. But this never works. Compelling statements come from someone who is making an original, sincere and precise observation.

I've seen people go away from Patrick's class and send clear and useful emails while others write entire books.

Lazy Hazy Language

Some of us are making language mud. "I am so totally sure that we might be able to do it, if we could like, get ahead."

We use wimpy words that don't stand up: We are "kind of" passionate. We make a commitment that we will be there, "hopefully."

We connect everything with filler: and, um, uh, you know, and, so, does that make sense?

These three fall under the category of what Patrick calls using "bad words." They are words that don't really mean anything. Or words that could mean so many things, we can't be sure what they mean.

Often, we apologize: "This is probably a dumb question, but; I'm not a good speaker; I'm sorry for being emotional."

Everything changes when your language is clear, candid and direct: "Here's our challenge; this is my suggestion; I believe; here's my experience; let's look at this square-on."

Words with Heat

Robert F. Kennedy, Jr. is a powerful, angry speaker. He stands tall, broad-chested and commanding. He uses his right hand to gesture like a conductor. His shocking message about the environment and his passion work in concert. He radiates heat. You don't just hear his brilliance. You feel his passion.

Do you carry a passage from your favorite poet that will be with you forever? Do you ponder the lyrics when you listen to songs? Do you stop to think about words that are so perfectly suited to say a thing that it IS the thing? Have you ever read something that resonated with you so deeply you could have written it?

> *Do not go gentle into that good night.*
> *Rage, rage against the dying of the light.*
> *—Dylan Thomas*

We're not suggesting that you recite poetry in your business presentations—or tap into your angry passion—although much worse offenses are created by Sophisticated Bull. We are suggesting that you drop the clutter and use words that are meaningful to you—speak about those things that make you animated and alive.

Devil Slides

It is very popular to bash and trash PowerPoint® today, and there are lots of tips on how to avoid the evil "text shows." But using slides more effectively is useless until we address the real culprit, which is the *inauthentic speaker.*

Simple, beautiful visual aids help develop understanding and retention. Garr Reynolds has written the best book on design principles for presentations out there. Consider picking up a copy of *Presentation Zen.*

We have to be courageous enough to make a stand for common sense. Refuse to allow your name to be associated with lifeless slides. There are too many talented people who can augment your message through striking design.

PRACTICE 7
TAKE LEAPS

It's not as far as you think.

When it's time to stand up and be the center of attention, do you feel a surge of nervousness and adrenaline? Good. This means you are fully aware of the opportunity and when you leap, if you leap, you will meet your greatness.

Elvis Presley said this about it: "I've never gotten over what they call stage fright. I go through it every show... It's a new crowd out there, it's a new audience, and they haven't seen us before. So it's got to be like the first time we go on."

Artists and athletes know that fear energizes a performance. We can take a page from their book. Because when it's channeled, that nervous energy is an unmatched source of vitality. Risk itself is connected to our greatness. If we have nothing to risk, we are lackluster and dull.

The challenge is not overcoming a fear of risk and public speaking. It is turning fear into energy. To speak to each group as though it were the first time.

When Jerry Seinfeld tells this fairly famous joke, "Most of us would rather be in our casket than give the eulogy at a funeral," he's referring to a survey in which Americans were asked to name their greatest fear.

Fear	
Public Speaking	42%
Fear of heights	32%
Insects	22%
Sickness	19%
Death	19%

Surveys like this have helped make speaking an enormous nightmare. Instead of singling out public speaking, I would prefer they measure the fear of looking bad in front of others.

Fear of public speaking is just one example of social phobia. Fear of public speaking is just a subset of the fear of looking bad in front of people who are making judgments. Social phobia is common and is thought to affect one in ten people at some time in their lives—in music recitals, art showings, dog shows, marathons, and yes, public speaking.

When I was seven years old, I was asked to give the blessing at a Thanksgiving table of 15 relatives. I began, "Now I lay me down to sleep," and the room erupted into hilarity. As you can tell, I never forgot it!

Most of us experience anxiety before speaking or presenting. But this rush of adrenaline does not mean you aren't doing a good job.

People generally don't believe this until they see a video of themselves. It is amazing that the effects of this performance anxiety—this heightened energy—are hidden from the audience. But they are. As viewers and listeners we see only a fraction of the symptoms; and once you relax into a conversation, we don't even remember them.

If you're like me, you have had a bad experience with choking. And what a terrible word that is. When we're not aware of it, adrenaline can take us by surprise. When we stand to speak, the primitive brain senses that the heart is exposed to the enemy tribe and we are at risk. (Never mind that tribes are millennia back on the evolutionary tree. Our instincts don't know that.) A gush of adrenaline provides the energy we could use to get the heck out of there. This does not feel good. We resist the sensation because most of the time, we're trying not to flee. We begin to second-guess what we're trying to say. We become concerned that we're looking bad. We start to use words like "um" a lot. The fear is on us. We're babbling. We're hesitating. We're going down in flames.

The Riddle

Researchers have attempted to solve the riddle of how intense speaker anxiety is consistently underestimated by such a large number of people observing it. In 1959, Theodore Clevenger first observed that speaker-reported and audience-observed anxiety operate at low levels of interdependence. Since then, a number of investigators have confirmed Clevenger's observation. Studies conducted in 1987, 1990, 1992 and 1996 have substantiated the tendency for audiences to miss anxiety states reported by speakers.

This is not your private boogeyman. It happens to everybody in one way or another. And there are easy ways to deal with it. Here is a process that will allow you to harness the energy of your adrenaline:

- Allow yourself to struggle before the talk. Practice out loud, on your feet. Feeling prepared and having muscle memory will settle you down.

- Identify your symptoms and watch for them. Every time I speak, my hands go clammy about 30 minutes out, like clockwork. I expect it. I am not surprised by it. Figure out what shows up first for you, such as weak knees, butterflies, palpitations or dry mouth.
- When the symptoms show up, say to yourself, "Oh, good. My energy is here." At first this might not feel true. Do it anyway. When your words travel on harnessed adrenaline, you are in your most powerful state. This allows you to throw lightning bolts of meaning—a powerful gift. Why would you want to resist this power? Welcome it.
- Don't memorize anything, but embrace your opening lines and know them so well that you can say them without thinking. This will help you push through the "adrenaline wall."
- Begin to observe your adrenaline experience. Just notice. Then, when you feel yourself begin to lose focus, make the decision to come back into the room and focus on your listeners. This takes a little practice but it is the key.
- Change your breathing habits. Breathe slowly through your nose, from the diaphragm. This crucial step is worthy of additional attention.

Life Habit: Diaphragm Breathing

In the West, we tend to take shallow breaths and practice chest breathing, which uses limited lung capacity. When you stand to speak, your chest can tighten, and suddenly there is just a small stream of oxygen going to the brain. We're out of air and can't pump enough in through the chest. This is a terrible sensation.

The diaphragm is the muscle wall between the chest and the abdomen. It's the major muscle we use in natural breathing. If you develop the habit of diaphragmatic breathing—not only when speaking and presenting but in everyday life—the benefits can be transformational.

Diaphragmatic breathing uses more lung capacity, sends more oxygen to the brain, relaxes the chest and releases your tone of voice and vocal volume. Here is a simple exercise to help you practice.

- Find the diaphragm. Lie on the floor, on your back. Place one hand on your chest, and the other on your stomach with little finger just above the naval. Breathe slowly and notice the movement. The movement should come only from your lower hand.
- Breathe into the diaphragm. Breathe through your nose. Your stomach should push out like a balloon. Once it is full, allow the balloon to slowly collapse. Let the air slowly out of your mouth as you continue pulling inward as far as it will go, until you have no breath left.
- Practice for a few minutes before you get out of bed in the morning and

when you get into bed at night. Breathe through your nose using the diaphragm, push out as far as you can. Hold for a couple of seconds before allowing the balloon to collapse. Increase the number of seconds you can leave the balloon full until you release the air.

There are folks who have acute social phobia and stage fright, such as Barbra Streisand, Donny Osmond and Kim Basinger, but they are in the minority. If you're like Elvis and the rest of us, adrenaline is a good thing. It kicks up the electricity in the room. It can be navigated. You can learn to enjoy it.

Adrenaline is also connected to inspiration and acts of courage. Have you ever experienced a crisis in which you acted without thinking?

"Dog Fight" Edited
Jeffrey C. Hart

Jeffrey Hart grew up on a farm in Kentucky, surrounded by animals—dogs, cats, pet turkeys, goats and a pet cow. "I am not ashamed to admit I like animals more than some people," he says.

His passion was tested a few years back in an incident involving his 85-pound black Lab named Cameron, and a 125-pound Rottweiler belonging to a neighbor. One day his neighbor was walking her Rottweiler and decided she would bring him into Jeff's backyard to play with Cameron.

Jeff was in the house and his wife was in the backyard when suddenly everything went terribly wrong. He heard the sound of the Rottweiler and knew he was going for Cameron's throat.

"The one thing you're not supposed to do is get in the middle of a dog fight," says Jeffrey, "but this Rottweiler was killing my dog." Jeffrey stormed into the backyard and dove between the dogs. He was pulling the Rottweiler off Cameron by his jaws, completely unaware of the wounds the dog was inflicting on him.

Once Jeffrey was able to release Cameron from the Rottweiler's jaws, neighbors scooped up the bleeding dog and rushed him to the emergency vet. As the dust settled, Jeffrey realized that he had puncture wounds all over his legs and side.

After backing into his neighbor's car as he backed down the drive, Jeffrey managed to drive himself to two different hospitals, where he was refused medical attention because he wouldn't turn in the dogs. Turning in the dogs could have meant they would be put to sleep. As a last resort, Jeffrey's brother, a doctor in Winston Salem, agreed to stitch him up in his kitchen.

The moral? You'll be surprised what passion (and adrenaline) can do.

The Center of Attention

I work with high school students who are participating in the International Baccalaureate (IB) program. We conduct a Communications Boot Camp for juniors and seniors that allows them to practice expressing their ideas and interviewing for scholarships. These students often have amazing bursts of authentic expression.

> There is the risk you cannot afford to take, and there is the risk you cannot afford not to take.
>
> – Peter Drucker

One fall, a young woman stood in the center of the room and said, "I am Russian." Not in a casual way, but as a way of standing for something.

"I am Russian. It is such a great part of me. I lived in Russia for 13 years. When I came here, I had been up-rooted. I didn't know anything, anyone, no one. America has become my country. But Russia, I am proud of it. It is me. Every single part of me—the language, the customs, has been Russian."

At 17, this speaker held the room in the palm of her hand. She was the center of attention, with tears in her eyes, trembling with adrenaline and strength.

> Be brave enough to live life creatively. The creative is the place where no one else has ever been. You have to leave the city of your comfort and go into the wilderness of your intuition. You can't get there by bus, only by hard work and risk and not quite knowing what you're doing. What you'll discover will be wonderful. What you'll discover will be yourself.
>
> – Alan Alda

"I went back to Russia this year. I had such a great experience with my friends. I miss them. America has become my country. But I want you all to know about Russia. I'm proud of its culture. It has layers. It has been there for so many centuries. So many customs, traditions. I don't want to keep Russia inside, I want to share it."

This young woman spoke for no more than two minutes and when she walked away we were all stunned. Too often when we become the center of attention, we hesitate and become self-conscious. But to become the center of attention and stand tall, now that's something.

The moment we become self-conscious, we fumble where we were flying. The Ego grows, the world shrinks and the air tightens. We become disconnected from the listeners and begin to wonder if we're looking bad. We fumble for words and spiral downward since we can only think of our own performance instead of being fully present in the moment with the audience and what we are trying to say.

It takes practice, but you can pull yourself out of self-consciousness. First, notice when this happens. When you feel yourself disconnect, gently focus and bring yourself back in to the room. Show up in your shoes and transmit your message to listeners. Say something directly to an individual in the group, as though you are the only two in the room. Tether yourself back into the conversation.

Your Topic

I believe everyone has a topic they care about and are uniquely qualified to speak about—and chances are, you are further along in uncovering your topic than you realize. It's with you now. What do you care about? Developing a Learning Culture? Lifestyle Classes after work? Re-Branding? Diversity? Family-friendly Work Environment? Improving meetings within the company? Going Green? A cause your organization can get behind?

Take up your topic. You will find it in four elements: unique ability; life experiences and lessons learned; acquired knowledge and skill; and passion and deep interests.

Many of us don't want to put ourselves on the line. The idea that some people are just not good at speaking is one I hear all the time. The other one is that some people don't need speaking skills in their work. These are excuses that reduce our magnificent ability to communicate to a job.

> A bit of advice to a young Native American at the time of his initiation: As you go the way of life, you will see a great chasm. Jump. It's not as far as you think.
>
> *— Joseph Campbell*

This has nothing to do with becoming a circuit speaker. It's about releasing and feeding your authenticity. Whether you run meetings, give seminars, make presentations or have high-stakes conversations, speaking on a topic you care about is worthy of your attention.

Don't Miss It

Don't miss what this is all about. The fear that surrounds public speaking is not that different from the fear that is deep within the human psyche: the fear that we will fail to meet the standard, look bad in front of others, stumble in public and be criticized as incompetent.

Authentic Speaking is not for the faint-hearted. It requires that you take risks, trust your originality, accept the gift of fear and take leaps.

Standing up to *Say Something Real* is transformative for you and for us. The moment you step from behind all the noise and talk about what is important to you, we all become better for it.

SECTION IV

SEVEN KEYS TO A CULTURE OF AUTHENTIC COMMUNICATION

If we are to better the future we must disturb the present. – Catherine Booth

I really love business when it's at its best. Business is part of our expression in the world. But you don't have to look very far to know it is time to disturb the present. We can't wait around for the world to change. The future economy is about you and me taking responsibility for the way we communicate.

Take Time for the Future

Authentic Communication is not just one of the most important core values of a business—it is undeniably the most direct way to harness trust and impact performance. The reason we don't know this is that we have been trapped in short-term gain, and we have deluded ourselves into thinking that we don't have time for the future.

7
Keys
to Building
a Culture of
Authentic
Communication

1 Know

2 Walk

3 Go Deep

4 De-Bull

5 Ask, Learn, Thrive

6 Foster Teams

7 Inspire

KEY 1
KNOW

To the person who does not know where he wants to go there is no favorable wind. —Seneca

The downfall of so many businesses is failing to keep it simple. Everyone in the organization should know two stories like the back of their hands: *Who We Are* and *What We Do.*

Denny Hammack learned how to inspire and include people as an athlete. Today he is the president and owner of Patterson Pope, a fast growth company in three states that offers storage products, storage space and document management. He and his management team have created a Culture of Authentic Communication.

Hammack believes that: "What you sell and where you sell it…are only pieces of it. How you carry it off, and who you carry it off with—that's the excitement."

Patterson Pope is headquartered in a sprawling state-of-the-art facility in Charlotte, North Carolina. Hammack and his partners have up-fitted the building with unique manufacturer showcases. The company's web site and video vignettes are edgy and fun.

As you walk through the main entrance, you know instantly that something different is going on—the interior colors, the unusual logo, the displays and the atmosphere of caring and ease. "There are no boring businesses," says Hammack, "only ones run by people who have allowed them to be boring."

Hammack invited two marketing experts, Calvin James and Patrick McLean, to conduct deep interviews and identify the Patterson Pope brand residing in the employees and clients. They began with a tag line.

"Space Made Simple," says Hammack. "This is what we do in three words. I used to have so much difficulty telling people what we did." From there, a *What We Do* statement was formed:

We make space and materials simple. If it's in your organization, and you can touch it, we help you store it, track it and retrieve it using less space and time than you ever thought possible.

"Branding is not just for our customers," says Hammack. "Our brand is also for our own people. Done rightly, marketing sustains excitement and pride for employees. And by keeping it fresh, we are telling people to stay tuned." Hammack is especially proud of the *Who We Are* statement for Patterson Pope:

We keep things simple. We tell the truth, we keep our word, we do the right thing—because it's simpler that way. People like us, trust us and buy from us because we are free from guile. We work hard, we have fun, we go home to our families. We keep things simple.

KEY 2
WALK

"Let's get together. I'll call you." Most of us have tossed around some hot air in our time. We may not mean to, but we say things and don't follow up.

Do people pay more attention to what you do, or what you say? Remember our old pal Albert Mehrabian? His study found that visual and vocal elements account for 93% of believability. That leaves just 7% for the verbal element. If I say, "I'm so excited," with a pan face, do you believe me?

It is believed that the followers of Aristotle discussed philosophy while walking about with him. Perhaps they were "Walking the Talk."

The concept of congruence in communication is when a person's internal beliefs and behaviors are in agreement. The individual's words, voice and body language all give the same message.

It has never been more important for business people to Walk the Talk. It's the core premise of authenticity. We have to declare who we are, and we have to be who we say we are.

Charlotteans have always taken pride in the fact that we are a city of volunteerism and giving. So when a series of events at United Way of the Central Carolinas hit the headlines, emotions ran high. CEO Gloria Pace King, whose salary and retirement benefits were under scrutiny, was asked to resign.

King is a force—she has been working and making her way since she was 14 years old. She was one of the first African American women to attend the School of Nursing in Cleveland. She was one of the first African American RNs to run a major hospital emergency room. She advises others: "Own your reality and don't expect anyone else to do it for you."

King worked tirelessly to raise a half-billion dollars during her 14-year tenure as head of the United Way. No one disputes that. But amid reports of flamboyance in her dress and lifestyle, coupled with controversy over her pay and benefits, she became unpopular with the community.

When the press caught wind of King's salary coming in at more than $1.2 million last year, a closed-door tactic by the board made the story ignite. Reporters asked for copies of board meeting minutes, King's employment contract and her retirement plan contracts, and were told the documents were confidential.

The demise of so many organizations is failing to keep it simple, and Walk the Talk. At the heart of the United Way debacle is a gaping hole in communication. There was no genuine conversation between King and the community. There was no candid conversation between the board and the press.

King and members of the Board of Directors are good people who have worked hard on behalf of this community. It's a complicated story—but in the end, the public could not overlook the idea that they did not Walk the Talk. It's ironic that both King's success and departure have been driven by a fierce determination to succeed. Ultimately she became a liability to the agency; the Board of Directors asked for her resignation to restore public trust.

One observer writes on a local blog: "The real tragedy, of course, happens at the doors of 91 United Way agencies. Last year's campaign total might be a high-water mark for this year and years to come."

KEY 3
GO DEEP

Commitment is never an act of moderation. –Kenneth G. Mills

You cannot do this as an afterthought. The answer is to Go Deep and put your faith back into communication. This is not easy since the world seems to be going the other way.

Researchers have given us a boatload of evidence that trust is tied directly to performance. When trust is high, performance is multiplied. People offer ideas and learn together. When trust is low, people worry and revenues slip.

Don't we all know this? Trust is the lifeblood running through healthy businesses. But there's a catch. Trust requires something the business ego really hates: vulnerability.

> **Trust is one's willingness to be vulnerable to another person, based on the belief that the relationship is one of competence, openness, concern, and reliability.**
>
> *– A. K. Mishra*

Vulnerability is a big part of trustworthiness. So how do you go about building an environment of trust? Through Authentic Communication that allows people to be vulnerable with one another.

I cannot count the number of times I've coached an executive who showed up to practice a presentation on the company's future with dizzy flow charts and fat decks with crowded slides. The notion that this form of communication works is like *The Emperor's New Clothes*. Everyone knows it ain't so, but we play along.

Recently I worked with a brilliant man who carries the responsibility of being the spokesperson for a seismic initiative. Naturally any topic of such weight deserves a complicated presentation. Right? He came to our studio with a suitcase.

We put the suitcase aside and I asked him to simply tell me about the initiative. He is a fascinating man. At the end of the day we eliminated half of his slides, stripped out most of the copy, added photographs from the company archives. Most importantly we came up with a wonderful metaphor to wrap the new concept around, and we left room for his stories.

No way does all this replace analytical content. There will be times when this executive will teach three-hour sessions on his topic and he will need the suitcase. But more often he will be speaking to provide awareness of how this initiative fits into the big picture, and he can put most of the technical information in a separate document at the exit doors.

> **Extended trust requires that firms and individuals expose their vulnerabilities to one another.**
>
> *– George Brenkert*

Storytelling is stronger than mere words, since it opens up both the imagination and the intellect. In the feedback I receive from employees at dozens of client companies, personal storytelling by executives is helping employees let down their guard and trust the executive and the company.

Face-to-Face with the Human Moment

Don't blow off the raw, creative firepower of the Human Moment because we're flung about the globe. The lack of it gives rise to distrust among employees. Geographic separation is a staggering factor, but we can't use it as a blanket excuse to swallow a business world without it.

> **Face-to-Face presence**
>
> +
>
> **Authentic Communication**
>
> =
>
> **Complete Intellectual and Emotional Engagement**

> Human beings can deal with almost anything as long as they don't become too isolated… the Human Moment is defined as an authentic psychological encounter that can happen only when two people share the same physical space.
>
> *– Edward Howell*

We can do a much better job at providing face-to-face opportunities for the people in a single location. Researchers know that electronic communication does not build trust—but it can be fortified by some face-to-face contact.

We've been swimming around in murky business communication for so long that we overlook the possibility of clean water. Bottom line: Authentic Communication drives performance if you Go Deep and practice it company-wide. Is this a tall order? You bet.

KEY 4
DE-BULL

Genius means little more than the faculty of
perceiving in an unhabitual way. –William James

M ike Boykin runs the Charlotte division of a large sports marketing
firm that employs 75 energetic young people who work everything
from the NASCAR Nextel Cup Series to NFL games. Mike is
notorious for bringing fun into the work equation—including meetings.

New employees who are introduced at Mike's monthly staff meeting are
required to sing a few verses of a song of their choice. These performances
have become so popular that singers are showing up in full costume with
karaoke music. Other meeting segments feature non-traditional speakers on
little-known areas of the company (no boring updates are allowed).

Every organization should have a campaign led by the employees to scrap
bad meetings. Meet in different places. Take just ten minutes to meet, having
everyone weigh in on what's on their plate that day. When there's nothing to
meet about, don't meet.

Bad meetings are an incubator for Sophisticated Bull. For gargantuan
results, take up this cause. Cut meeting times in half. Tolerate no interruption
by phone calls or e-mails. Start on time. End on time. Meet for five minutes
while standing.

We have surrendered to the necessary evil of bland teleconferences. These
calls are killing us. We drift and multi-task. We are tortured by monotone
speakers who talk non-stop.

Aren't we more creative than this? Great conference calls are possible.
Open the call with something brief, edgy and interesting. Make it some sort of
educational series for call participants only. Lay down the parameters of the
call and challenge everyone to make it happen with energy. Train everyone on
all the latest conferencing software and make the most of polling features for
feedback. Don't allow people to dial in if they're in the building—have them
stand with you for the call.

Start a De-Bull campaign. Put everyone in the organization on watch. Create a company manifesto and post it on a private page of the website. Have employees cast their votes for what to ban:

- Blackberry prayer position in meetings
- Complicated vision statement
- No training and development
- "This is the way we've always done it"
- Bad-mouthing clients
- Long, draining, bad meetings
- Being late all the time
- Hoarding information
- Playing it safe
- Vague, soupy messages
- Low standards
- Lightweight presentations
- Boring slides
- Fear of failure (no lessons learned)
- Bragging, interrupting
- Low-risk competence
- Facts without what the facts mean
- No questions asked
- Quick consensus without healthy debate
- Low self-awareness
- Slow, junky communication procedures
- No flexibility
- No inspiration
- Staying in the problem instead of moving to solution

The only folks who can de-bull your business are your employees. At this very moment, they can tell you what is holding them back. Go ask them.

KEY 5
Ask, Learn, Thrive

"Personal development" sounds too casual and wimpy for the phenomenal process it represents. Awareness is the one true game-changer an individual can sustain in life. Cultures of Authentic Communication provide opportunities for personal development.

As a boy, Einstein was in trouble all the time because the teachers accused him of asking stupid questions. Once everyone knew he was brilliant, he could ask whatever he liked.

Have you ever been reluctant to ask a question? As a leader, do you welcome questions as a sign of engagement?

It takes a leader to promote learning and the art of asking great questions—they have a way of searing through Sophisticated Bull.

Why don't we ask more questions? Mick Mixon believes that people have become afraid to give the impression that they don't already know everything.

> The important thing is not to stop questioning. Curiosity has its own reason for existing. One cannot help but be in awe when he contemplates the mysteries of eternity, of life, of the marvelous structure of reality. It is enough if one tries merely to comprehend a little of this mystery every day. Never lose a holy curiosity.
>
> – Albert Einstein

"I love asking questions," says Mixon, "People think I'm a little weird. That's okay. I used to tell my students, not to be afraid to ask the non-traditional questions. Sportswriters often try to pass statements off as questions, such as, Tiger, you've got to feel good about what you did out there today," in hopes that the subject will just catch on and begin talking. That, to me, is unacceptable.

Don't be afraid to ask the courageous, thoughtful, creative, open-ended questions. If everyone in the room thinks you're a little different, too bad. You have to trust that your way is the right way. You'll raise the bar for everyone else who thinks that conversational pabulum is a five-course meal."

Confidence

In a project entitled "Catching Confidence," the National Institute of Adult Continuing Education found that confidence is a direct result of learning. Adults who had successfully learned something new experienced an increase in confidence and discovered new dreams and aspirations.

Learning does not require classrooms. Help people develop themselves. Match people to projects that will catch fire. Leaders can also encourage the investment by individuals in their own ideas. At times the only difference between exceptional and mediocre is the courage to make a stand for an idea.

Recently I heard H. A. "Humpy" Wheeler, former president of Lowe's Motor Speedway, speak to a group of entrepreneurs. Wheeler made his name as one of NASCAR's most creative promoters. He told us that the greatest practice to innovation is to open your door wide to every employee with an idea, from bad to brilliant, and celebrate each one.

Invest in learning. Make educational budgets available. Invite people to reflect on "What do I do best? What do I want to be?" People who stay involved with these questions and set goals have a visible measure of passion. The more people expand, the less they are threatened and the more freedom they have to innovate.

Help People Transform Themselves

In *Re-imagine!* Tom Peters writes that leaders don't transform employees, people transform themselves. But leaders can offer people chances to learn, explore, invent and win. Leaders can help people catch fire with the right projects.

At Patterson Pope, Denny Hammack is focused on recruiting and nurturing great talent. The interview process is long but energetic. The management team takes an avid interest in every single employee—and makes it a goal for each one to thrive in the role to which they are most suited, and to experience what they call "big wins."

As a result, Patterson Pope has become a magnet for talent. "Today, people want more than a paycheck. They want to be a part of something bigger," says Hammack. "They want to thrive."

So how might you allow employees to thrive? Ask them. Start a brainstorm list: lifestyle seminars, lunch and learns, cross-training, personal education accounts, speaker bureaus, etc.

KEY 6
FOSTER TEAMS

None of us is as smart as all of us. –Ken Blanchard

My last stint in broadcasting was a sweet and prolific run with a group of people I loved then and still love today. We knew who we were and what we did. We shared integrity and trust and we did extraordinary work.

> All truly great minds have been reinforced through contact with others that allowed them to grow and expand.
>
> *– Napoleon Hill*

Somewhere along the line business leaders have allowed the ability to forge interpersonal relationships to slip down the priority list. Here's what the academics have been telling us: people who are allowed to build community in small work groups will do amazing things. They will perform better and faster. They will be more creative and innovative.

Nothing lights up your brain cells like problem solving with smart people you trust. Today I have a network of brainstorm buddies. We are wired together by passion and a caring for one another's success.

Jeff Bezos of Amazon came up with the notion of the "two-pizza team." If you can't feed a team with two pizzas, it's too large. That limits a task force to five to seven people, depending on their appetites.

Amazon's pizza teams have created some of the site's most popular features. They conceived of the Gold Box, a little animated icon of a treasure chest that gleams and wobbles at the top of Amazon's home page. A click to "open" the box reveals special offers that last for just an hour from the time of the click.

Face-to-face communication is still the most powerful medium for explaining complex ideas, brainstorming and getting buy-in; it also grows trust.

Long before Bezos, Napoleon Hill studied more than 700 successful people to learn their secrets of success. In *Think and Grow Rich*, he wrote about master-mind groups.

He defined a master-mind group as "coordination of knowledge and effort, in a spirit of harmony, between two or more people for the attainment of a definite purpose."

Enlightened leaders make it easy for people to work in small teams or form master-mind groups. A small group of people who are connected to one another and the big picture can do anything.

Key 7
INSPIRE

The companies that survive longest are the ones that work out what they uniquely can give to the world—not just growth or money but their excellence, their respect for others, or their ability to make people happy. Some call those things a soul.–Charles Handy

In 1982 the late Paul Newman began the Newman's Own brand, selling pasta sauces, microwaveable popcorn and the like. When the profits began kicking in, he decided to begin a camp in Connecticut for kids with cancer, AIDS and other blood-related diseases. He built the camp to look like a Western town and named it the Hole in the Wall Camp from Butch Cassidy. He had a vision for a camp that would eventually provide one counselor for every two kids.

Newman's Own became a monster success, launching an organic line run by Paul's daughter and by 2002, donating over $125 million to charity. Newman remained humble and joked, "the embarrassing thing is that my salad dressing is now out-grossing my films."

> Upon hearing a little girl say how much she cherished his camp, Paul Newman said, "That's the applause. That's what you really want in life."

Paul Newman was a Renaissance man who remained humble. He will be remembered for his acting career—but even more for his humanity.

Business is Not Separate

A good bit of low performance is the result of milking the market for what's good for the company. The future is about making a contribution to the world.

I have gone back to graduate school and a fringe benefit comes from attending classes with amazing 20-somethings who have a completely different orientation to life.

> **Spiritual capital reflects what an individual or an organization exists for, believes in, aspires to, and takes responsibility for.**
>
> *– Danah Zohar*

The young people I know want more than a paycheck. They want a family life and flexibility at work; and they want to be vision-led and values-led by a leader who is interested in whether or not the world needs a particular product. They are looking for "servant leaders" who are in touch with the planet. They are looking for inspiration.

Does this sound like a non-business message? Business is not separate from life. The two are interwoven. It is a great mistake to think there's no bottom line in all this. Uninspired people are the most costly and dangerous expense to your business.

SECTION V

MORE STORYTELLING ARTISTS

I believe we are longing for dignity and daring. What if we were to risk authenticity in business, not only to become more prosperous, but to create more of the life we want? What is work if it isn't, at its core, creative?

Whether we realize it or not, the thirst for creative expression is a heat source in our lives. I believe we can renew our faith in Authentic Communication and begin to create more of what we want. We can begin with the relevance we create for others when we tell what life has taught us—when we tell our stories.

> Real art has
> the capacity to
> make us nervous.
>
> – *Susan Sontag*

"Frustrated Artist"
Lou Solomon

I have a picture of me and Alan Jackson in my office. It's there to remind me, every time I see it, that I am an artist.

I met Alan Jackson in 1986 when he was just a tall, lanky fellow from Georgia working in the mailroom of the Nashville Network. In those days I was too busy getting it right and plotting my next promotion to invest in friendships or put any faith in people who came from the lowly mailroom. But Alan was funny and friendly with a sideways grin. He made me laugh.

One day he said to me, "You know, this is just a temporary job. I've got a recording contract and it looks like they're going to make me a star."

"Oh," I said, rolling my eyes, "you're a frustrated artist." I judged Alan to be like every valet parker, busboy and waitress in Nashville. They're all looking for stardom. Inwardly I thought, "Oh brother." Alan paused for a moment, looked me straight in the eye and said, "Well, I guess we're all frustrated artists."

By '89 I had moved to Charlotte, North Carolina, to work for WSOC-FM and Cox Broadcasting. Our morning man, the late Bill Dollar, walked out of the studio and tossed me the new *Radio & Records*, an industry publication. On the bottom of the front page there was a banner ad that read: "Arista Records presents Alan Jackson!"

In '90 I attended the Country Radio Seminar at the Opryland Hotel in Nashville. On the first evening I saw Alan standing side stage at the New Faces Showcase and made my way over to him. There he was. They damn sure had made him a star.

> **I am not a businessman.**
> **I am an artist.**
>
> *– Warren Buffett*

Following is a delicious slice of the stories from a few of the artists who have come through my studio.

"Life is Not Set in Concrete" Unedited
Janet England

"I was anchoring the six o'clock news when razor sharp pains jabbed my stomach like an ice-pick. I could tell I was beginning to bleed and knew it could be serious. I was pregnant. My husband was alerted and as the newscast ended he carried me from the studio. My doctor told him to take me to the hospital. Through the night, medicine tried to save our baby, but morning brought the dreaded words: 'Janet, it's nature's way. You've had a miscarriage.'

'Nature's way!' my mind screamed. I was angry at their words. This was my child, our child. It was growing inside of me for three months. We would never see our baby in this lifetime. Everyone was kind, sorry, patting my hand and saying, 'life goes on.' It did and so did the pain and anger.

Many couples suffer miscarriages, but it was the mid-eighties and the topic wasn't discussed much. 'Nature's way,' was the common explanation and if you were fortunate, like I was, you could try again. That was it. Get over it. Move on. My husband and I rarely talked about it. He thought bringing it up would upset me. I couldn't talk about it, and wondered why he didn't. We each felt frustrated, alienated from each other. Someone suggested a grief counselor.

Mary, the physiologist, had a quiet face with warmth shining from her eyes. She gave us permission to grieve alone and together as a couple. During this process to healing, I mentioned that I sometimes felt fearful, paralyzed, and unable to make decisions. She told me these important words: 'Life is not set in concrete. Make decisions based on what you know…now. Later, make another decision based on new information.'

Even now, twenty-some years later, when I say the words, stress falls from my body. Situations in life will cause pain, fear and confusion. Life is a journey. Love and faith will move us forward out of those hard, rocky places to the next step…and the next step…in our lives."

"Stand Your Ground" Edited
Roger Sarow

"Stand Your Ground" is a legal clause that means the shooter has no duty to abandon personal property, or to give up ground to an assailant.

There are colorful characters in our past—people whose stories are forever catalogued in our brain. Roger Sarow told us about a former colleague:

"I'm thinking of a man who had a real impact on my life. His name is Ron Bornstein, long since retired," says Sarow, "Ron was Executive Director of Wisconsin Public Television and Radio back when I was an employee there in the 1970s and 80s.

Ron was a force. He was very aware of his craft, astute about the power of public broadcasting—and he was just tougher than hell. One day he advised me, 'When you've been around for a long time, you'll make a lot of friends, and you'll also make enemies. Be ready for that and stand your ground.'

Now Ron stood maybe 5'5". He was precisely dressed. He was the smallest guy in the room, but he delighted in taking on the biggest character he could find.

What I found out was that Ron had been the smallest kid in his neighborhood—on the wrong side of the tracks. He had gone through life standing his ground... I'll never forget him."

"No Pain, No Gain" Edited
Andy Dinkin

Like any other boy in the D.C. area, Andy Dinkin grew up following the Redskins. His family had no roots in athletics but Dinkin had promise as an athlete.

> There are no traffic jams along the extra mile.
>
> – *Roger Staubach*

When his parents divorced, Dinkin floundered until he found his way into the weight room in junior high. "I read every issue of *Muscle & Fitness Magazine* from cover to cover," says Dinkin. "I clipped the words 'No Pain, No Gain' and put them on the ceiling above my bed."

At age 14, Dinkin donned his first set of football pads. At practice, he worked harder than the other boys. After practice, he ran extra sprints and stayed late in the weight room. He wasn't encouraged at home. "I didn't come from a football family," says Dinkin. "They didn't really understand." But he dug down into himself and pulled up the inspiration to push, as though there were a coach constantly at his shoulder.

In his junior year of high school, Dinkin became a star defensive lineman, often featured in *The Washington Post* high school sports section. He was in top shape, weighing in at 230 pounds. "It became evident that I was going to be offered a scholarship," says Dinkin. "After graduation I took my five official visits to Maryland, Alabama, Penn State, Virginia Tech and Chapel Hill."

He chose Chapel Hill and went there with high expectations. But in his freshman year, Dinkin experienced his greatest challenge. During summer camp he took a hit to his knee, which put him in a cast for six weeks. A broken thumb and changes on the coaching staff made things worse. Suddenly he had lost his momentum and the new coaches didn't know him.

"The idea of going to Carolina on scholarship and not making a real contribution was unacceptable," says Dinkin. "College football is hard. You work out until you get sick and your body is always beat up. But I knew it was now or never. I dug in and played as though my life depended on winning. I started my last three seasons at Carolina."

Today Dinkin heads up business development for an innovative downtown mixed-use project. He is a husband, father and chairman of the Board of Directors for the non-profit, Girls on the Run. And in this part of the country, he will always be recognized as the defensive lineman and letterman of UNC Chapel Hill. In those moments he is reminded of the 14-year-old who stayed late in the weight room. In those moments he is reminded of the raw power of a committed soul.

"Photograph" Edited
Simone Orendain

Family photos can be found in every home, and there is a story behind each one. The nostalgic, black and white photos seem to draw us in to wonder about the faces, frozen in time.

Simone Orendain spoke to us while holding a framed family photograph from the '50s. Pointing, she said, "This is my mother. This is my grandmother, who died when my mom was 14."

With a catch in her throat, she continued, "When I went to the Philippines I got to know members of my mom's family that I didn't remember from the little time I had there growing up. I went to my great uncle's home. He was turning 95 and almost beyond speaking. He couldn't quite make the connection of who I was. I went up the stairs of my great uncle's old house and the walls were covered with old photographs. We got to this photo; he smiled and gestured, 'That's you.' I stood there feeling such a connection to my mother. He could see the resemblance."

When Orendain left the Philippines, she kept thinking about the photograph, and regretted that she had been too shy to ask for it. Years later, she is holding that photo like a treasure, a part of her identity.

We find our roots in the faces we favor in old back and white photographs. In a smile or the tilt of the head—we find ourselves.

"Building Up" Edited
Cynthia Carlson

Cynthia Carlson is pure moxie. She built two successful businesses in separate industries in Charlotte, North Carolina. She is an award-winning entrepreneur—and an intuitive connector of people to opportunity.

Twenty-five years ago, Carlson was a new business owner when a competitor managed to steal proprietary information—and rush to market with it. Betrayal is a devastating experience. It pulls the wind out you. Carlson spoke with her attorney, who knew they had the grounds to go to court.

> **What you resist persists.**
>
> – *Carl Jung*

But taking legal action would have been an exhausting act of resistance. Carlson had a thoughtful conversation with a good friend and member of her Board of Advisors. Her friend urged her to use her energy for "building up—not fighting, resisting and burning down."

"She gave me some of the best advice I've ever received," says Carlson. The outcome? Carlson's company became the largest privately-held technology training company in the southeast. The other firm was never a factor.

"A Dollar" Unedited
Thomas C. Williams

"Dr. Hunt Williams was my grandfather, my father's father. He lived until he was 99. An amazing man. A delightful and funny man. I didn't know him in his profession because he retired at the age of 72 and I had just been born; but he was a physician and a health commissioner in public health. He thought being a public servant was a good and noble profession. He had a few key sayings in life. He said he used to pay a man a dollar a year to do all of his worrying. What he was saying is, 'Don't worry—it's unproductive. Let it go. Set yourself free.' I worry too much. I need to find that man."

"Atonement" Edited
Eddie Link

Eddie Link is a bank executive. He is also a storyteller and a passionate historian. One of his private stories is about a 74-year-old veteran, a 7-year-old girl and Pearl Harbor.

In 1994 Link decided to take his entire family—his wife and three sons—to Hawaii. When he began the initial planning he decided to invite his father-in-law, Everett.

Everett is a WWII vet and was stationed at Pearl Harbor in 1941, at the time of the attack. He had not been back since his discharge from the Navy. Link, being an avid reader of WWII history, was hoping that Everett would open up and share what happened from a personal perspective. But Everett refused to even talk about the trip.

> A good head and a good heart are always a formidable combination.
>
> – Nelson Mandela

Three weeks before the trip Link received a call from his minister, Reverend Thompson, a U.S. Navy Reserve Chaplain. He said, "Your father-in-law needs to see the WWII Memorial. I will convince him to take the trip."

The first day in Hawaii they decided to do the climb up to Diamond Head, which is the volcano that overlooks Waikiki Bay. Climbing up, they were joined by a Japanese family on the trail—and an energetic little girl who was seven. When they got to the top of Diamond Head, they found gun boxes from the war that still overlook the bay. The little girl wanted to get up on top of one of the boxes and couldn't climb. Everett walked over and lifted her up on the gun box for this gorgeous view.

"They started talking, this 7-year-old child and 74-year-old man," said Link. "On the way back down, Everett watched the family quietly. Later he commented, 'how kind they seemed.'"

The next day the family went to the memorial. The only part run by the U.S. Navy is the launch that takes visitors from the museum out to the U.S.S. Arizona Memorial. Everett was quiet.

The launch is commanded by a full captain, which is a big deal. Captains command ships, not launches. On the ride over the captain got on the intercom and asked if there were any WWII vets on board, and if so, would they please stand. Four or five gentlemen—all 70 to 80 years old—stood, including Everett. When the Captain asked if any of them had survived Pearl Harbor, Everett was the only one left standing. The Navy Captain walked out to Everett and saluted saying, "Thank you for serving your country."

"Everett began to cry, and to let go of all the pain and loss," said Link. "We all cried with him—everyone on board. But the healing had begun the day before, on the top of Diamond Head, with a conversation between a 74-year-old veteran and a 7-year-old girl."

"Moments" Unedited
Jorge Fernandez

"My young friend Andrew is heading out on his odyssey next week, bound for Colorado. I am reminded of a time when I was not much younger than Andrew.

I was living in Miami when it became increasingly evident that it was time to think of college. It was 1979. I made a map and planned my road trip. In planning a trip like this you start building up a sense of excitement, a sense of anticipation and nervousness.

> Life is not measured by the number of breaths we take, but by the moments that take our breath away.
>
> – George Carlin

As I was going up the eastern seaboard, my senses were turned up a notch. These stops were all familiar to me. But when I headed west toward Minneapolis it became edgy. These were interesting times.

One night I stopped at a motel in Ohio. I drove a Volkswagen Rabbit and I was covered in soot from driving all day with the windows down. I got some fast food and watched a pre-season football game between the New England Patriots and the Green Bay Packers. I knew there was something exciting around the corner.

The next day I arrived in Minneapolis where for the following four years I went to college—and was sideswiped by waves of fortune Stephen Hawking could not calculate.

As I think of Andrew heading off, I am reminded of that trip and how important it is to keep your eyes and ears open. These are interesting times and interesting moments. Don't miss it, Andrew."

"Born to Run Businesses" Edited
David Stollmack

"A lot of people have great ideas," says David Stollmack, "but they let people talk them out of it. My first business was dubbing albums onto 8-track tapes in college. I had no idea it wasn't legal. I charged a dollar and twenty-five cents per tape."

Many businesses later, Stollmack just launched his third retail business, in home entertainment, Experience. He built the last business, Audio Video Systems, into an enterprise with three locations. He sold that business to a national chain and didn't plan on opening another store, but he couldn't stand it.

"I've watched where the business is going, and it's so exciting," says Stollmack. His new store resembles a design center with ways to include home entertainment in your home and in your lifestyle.

What drives him? Stollmack is an entertainment junkie. When a new film is released, he is there on the opening night. He is a one-man

Ticketmaster, trading and buying tickets to every event in Charlotte and beyond. He scours the paper for reviews or plays and restaurants. He has seen Bruce Springsteen in concert more than any other human being on the planet—70 times!

"I love the actual experience of entertainment and what it does to the senses," says Stollmack, "and my passion is sharing it with others. If someone stands in my store and smiles because they just experienced something new, I'm happy. You do it for the benefit of others. Then business is a joyful expression.

Entrepreneurs lead with our hearts as well as our heads. We see the market as a place of possibility; and more reasons as to why something will work than not work."

"Coach Shep" Edited
Terri Murphy

The high school stadium in Churchill, Maryland was recently dedicated to "Coach Shep," the beloved nickname of Fred Shepherd during his 27-year career of coaching football at Churchill High.

Coach Shep was not an easy coach. He pushed his players and his staff. He was demanding and he was a stickler for excellence. He taught principles: family and school work are first; winners train the hardest; games are won in the off-season; visualize your goals everyday; do the little things right; and give it all you've got.

But Coach Shep had much more than a knack for discipline. "He could see unique ability and pull it out of his players," says daughter Terri Murphy.

Think beyond your lifetime if you want to accomplish something truly worthwhile.

– Walt Disney

"He was tough—but his strength was in how much he cared. He really loved his students and his players." Murphy should know. Coach Shep nurtured her into a scholarship gymnast who lettered at Michigan all four years.

Coach Shep was inducted to the Maryland High School Football Hall of Fame in 1999. Murphy recites her dad's record easily: "He had 208 wins, 80 losses and 1 tie. He won 14 regional championships—he made it to the finals eight times and captured two state championships."

More impressive is that one man can influence so many lives. Former players will tell you that Coach Shep was a father figure. Others say they've raised their children on his principles and have been active in coaching young people. Over 200 of his players went on to play college football with 9 players reaching the NFL.

At the dedication, there was a gathering of former players, staff and students going back to the Class of '77. "It was such a sight," says Murphy. "All these grown men were tearing up and hugging my dad."

Coaches and mentors like Fred Shepherd make a stand for their players and students when they don't understand their potential. Coaches and mentors create a better future for us all.

"Teacher" Edited
Catherine A. Little

Children suffer their youth—wanting so badly to be regarded as adults. The respect shown by an adult can linger forever.

Dr. Philippe Martinez and his wife Olga were godparents to Catherine Little.

Martinez was a brilliant, gentle man—a professor of anatomy at Georgetown University. When most adults would shun the intrusion of a child into an artist's studio, he welcomed her and spoke to her about her interest in drawing and sketching.

"I loved to watch him paint using a palette knife," says Little. "The paint was thick and could be smeared or dabbed. I was so intrigued."

Dr. Martinez was in exile from Cuba. He not only welcomed Little into the studio but he told her about his homeland. He spoke to her person-to-person, and not adult to child. "He gave me that first nudge, that first encouragement," says Catherine. "He never shut me out of that world he so enjoyed, but engaged me and brought me in."

Often people are unaware of a unique moment they created for another human being. We all have experienced mentors who, in a very important moment or time, did or said something that touched us.

> **I've learned that people will forget what you said, people will forget what you did, but people will never forget how you made them feel.**
>
> *– Maya Angelou*

"It's Up to You" Edited
Ellison Clary

Ellison "Elly" Clary is a PR consultant and former speechwriter for Hugh McColl, former CEO of Bank of America. Elly once told me about a friend named Pat who made an impression on him early in his career. This is the way he described him:

"Pat was in charge of the posting room. Newspapers don't have posting rooms any more. Pat was rail thin…skinny. He had a false plate on his upper, and he was forever pushing it up. He had this big, booming voice. He was always strutting around the posting room, announcing deadlines. Pat liked his beer, and he especially liked bars. He was unseemly in a lot of ways…but what I learned from Pat was that unseemly or not, you can be comfortable in your skin. It's really up to you."

How I would have been cheated if Ellison said only that he worked with someone who ran the posting room who was quite a character.

"Generations" Edited
David L. Little, Jr.

In *The Greatest Generation*, Tom Brokaw wrote about the Americans who not only fought in World War II but watched over America during it. The people who raised this generation were the Depression Era folks who understood scarcity.

David Little told us a story about his granddad, who was a pharmacist in a small town in Mississippi. David spent every Christmas eve with his grandparents. The family tradition was to have a big meal, which was always quail, and open presents afterward.

"Invariably, every Christmas eve there would come a knock on the door. It was always someone from a poor family who had a sick child who had no other way to get care.

Granddaddy would put on his coat, go down to the drugstore and give them something. As often as not, he didn't charge them, which drove my grandmother insane, because she was in charge of the books, the money and the household. Money wasn't an issue for Granddaddy. He was one of the greatest people I ever knew. He lived the value of putting others before your own needs."

> **To be persuasive we must be believable; to be believable we must be credible; to be credible we must be truthful.**
>
> *– Edward R. Murrow*

"The Client is Not Always Right" Edited
Sally Mitchener

Sally Mitchener built a career managing dozens of top-performers. Before she left broadcasting she was director of sales for the six radio stations in the CBS/Infinity Group of Charlotte, North Carolina.

Twenty-five years ago, she was hired as a salesperson for a radio station in Raleigh, North Carolina, and was working diligently to learn the business and do everything right. Early on she experienced an upset with an important client who threatened to cancel his annual contract; and she discovered the ad agency executive had blamed her for a huge agency error.

"My teammates advised me to fall on my sword and make excuses since the agency represented so many station clients," says Mitchener. "In sales, the seller often bites the bullet and takes the fall to play nice, keep the peace, and save the business. But this is unhealthy for the business and the relationship. It's inauthentic."

Mitchener wasn't comfortable with the advice. She had a conversation with a good friend, Bev, who said: "Don't take the fall. The client is not always right."

Mitchener got in her car that same day and visited the client for a face-to-face conversation. She was calm, confident and honest about where the mistakes had been made. In the end, her relationships and her reputation were strengthened.

"Bev's advice stuck with me," says Mitchener. "Whenever there's a conflict in business or in life, the answer is face-to-face straight talk."

"Your Story" Edited
Mick Mixon

When asked what advice he would give business people preparing for an important presentation, Mick says this:

> The story of your life is not your life. It is your story. It is your personal narrative that matters, not the mere facts of your life.
>
> – John Barth

1. Connect a human story to any business presentation and you stand a good chance of relating to your audience.
2. Don't skimp on the detail. A good story can't be skeletal. It needs flesh. It needs color and texture.
3. Take a chance. State your feelings. Do something different. Get better at saying things like "thank you", "I'm sorry" and "I respect and admire what you do."
4. Develop the courage to ask meaningful, creative, open ended questions and then listen aggressively to the answers.
5. Waiting is an insult to those who have run out of time.

EPILOGUE
MY STORY

Lou Solomon

I was born into the era of Barbie, Lassie and Sugar Pops. My mother used to tell me about all the perfectly glamorous movie stars of her generation. There was a sigh in her voice when she said names like Ingrid Bergman and Humphrey Bogart.

But things weren't perfect in our home. I was the youngest child in a military household run by discipline, fear and violence. I lived in terror of my father, a complicated man we called "The Colonel."

Things weren't perfect in the world, either. The trail of assassinations and riots that pierced the '60s made people angry and cynical. I was 10 when the country watched the Vietnam War on the 6 o'clock news.

My solution in life was to be the perfectly behaved child who made perfect grades and spoke very little. The more perfect, the less reason for discipline. The less said, the fewer opportunities to be wrong. It seemed to work.

Women were second class inside my home, but they were emboldened on the outside in the '70s. Gloria Steinem had given us a new moniker ("Ms.") that didn't have anything to do with marital status. Billy Jean King beat Bobby Riggs and demanded equal purses for women athletes. I counted the days until I could escape to college and start a career.

The year I graduated from high school, Nixon was impeached. I remember Dan Rather reporting live, with the White House behind him. That image stuck with me. I longed to be in broadcasting, where people made a difference.

In college my heroes were Bob Woodward and Carl Bernstein of *The Washington Post*. I wrote with passion for my campus newspaper. I got my degree in Journalism and Communications and found a career in radio and television in Music City, USA, Nashville, Tennessee. Broadcasting was big and alive and I loved it.

I was an overnight workaholic. I fooled myself and everyone else into believing I was the bullet-proof rising star of broadcast marketing. But I had begun drinking back in high school and it escalated after college. I thought

I just loved happy hour and nightlife with friends, but I was medicating. Underneath it all I was a ticking time bomb of anxiety.

In the late '80s I hit bottom with alcoholism and exhaustion. I made the decision to enter rehab, with the support of my boss, family and close friends. It was nothing short of a near death experience, and my life has never been the same. I began this amazing trek toward my true work. I am comfortable in my skin, which is a miraculous state of being.

If you are struggling, have faith that you will pull a drawstring through this experience to shape who you are. Never settle for anything less than being who you are and saying that which is yours to say.

In the '90s I left broadcasting to become a PR consultant and eventually began to teach courses in public speaking. People came to these classes buried in their business personae. They came to learn techniques that would help them to be a "better speaker" but had no idea how to speak from the heart. In 2000, I founded Interact Skills, to teach Authentic Communication in business.

I have been sober since 1989. I have reconciled my life—the good and bad— and found my purpose. I am a writer and a speaker. But first and foremost, I am a teacher. I am absolutely clear on what my life has prepared me to do. When an individual stands in my studio and speaks from "the one who really is," the world stands still for both of us.

I won't tell my personal story all the time, and neither will you. But when it's time to tell it (and you will know), don't shrink from it.

> *There is something in every one of us*
> *that waits and listens for*
> *the sound of the genuine in ourselves.*
> *–Howard Thurman*

Seven Practices of Authentic Speaking

Practice 1: *Show Up*

When you take the front of the room—or begin a conversation—don't rush to speak. Stop and focus. As you break the "speed habit," you might feel uncomfortable, but you will learn to become more available. You can establish a connection in those first moments and set a tone for genuine exchange.

Practice 2: *Learn and Let Go*

We are not after technique—we are after your awareness. The danger of learning technique without letting go is that these techniques can become junk food for your inner critic.

Instead of being in the moment, you are worried about not doing it "right." Learn your instrument and then let go—and play soulfully.

Practice 3: *Focus Outward*

A good bit of human pain is the result of self-obsession. When we try to understand the world from the within, we create anxiety over looking bad. We disconnect and begin to obsess about our performance. The answer is to focus outward, on the listeners, and speak to them in earnest. Then we are free from self-obsession—free to connect.

Practice 4: *Allow Silence*

Silence holds enough power to say everything, if you allow it to. This is not easy. Silence requires the unthinkable—to do nothing, to just be in the moment. Too much talk can actually create stress for listeners. Natural spontaneity springs from silence. It provides a break in the action where someone might say something that is born of that very moment.

Practice 5: *Speak Story*

It's a crying shame that business people feel ill equipped to tell stories—and think storytelling is some sort of hybrid way of communicating. We don't have to work hard to rediscover the language of story. If anything, we have to stop making the idea so complicated. The most effective communication of your career and your life will emerge through storytelling.

Practice 6: *Design Simplicity*

All our lives we've been told to keep it simple. Why is this so hard to understand? Why instead do we insist on piling information on people? A Design for Simplicity is the creative approach that liberates Authentic Speaking and Presenting.

Practice 7: *Take Leaps*

Ultimately, you must make a courageous decision to leap out of your limitations—and be yourself. Take a chance. Say what you really think. Tell us how you feel. Authentic Speaking requires that you trust your originality and risk being misunderstood. It demands your greatness.

Seven Keys to a Culture of Authentic Communication

Key 1: *Know*

The downfall of so many businesses is failing to keep it simple. Everyone in the organization should know two stories like the back of their hands: *Who We Are* and *What We Do*.

Key 2: *Walk*

"Let's get together. I'll call you." Most of us have tossed around some hot air in our time. Maybe we don't mean to, but we say things and don't follow up. It has never been more important for business people to Walk the Talk. It's a core premise of authenticity. We have to *know* who we are and *be* who we say we are.

Key 3: *Go Deep*

Authentic Communication requires faith and deep commitment when the world seems to be going the other way. Bottom line: Authentic Communication drives performance if you Go Deep and practice it company-wide. Is this a tall order? You bet.

Key 4: *De-Bull*

Start a De-Bull Campaign. The folks who can de-bull your business are your employees. At this very moment, they can tell you what is holding them back. Go ask them. Number one on the list? Scrap bad meetings. Bad meetings are killing us.

Key 5: *Ask, Learn, Thrive*

"Personal development" sounds too wimpy for the phenomenal process it represents. Awareness is the one true game-changer an individual can sustain in life. Cultures of Authentic Communication encourage personal development.

Key 6: *Foster Teams*

It's unfortunate that somewhere along the line we allowed the ability to forge interpersonal relationships slip down the priority list. Here's what the academics have been telling us for a while: people who are allowed to build community in small work groups will become high performance teams and push your organization into a competitive edge.

Key 7: *Inspire*

A good bit of low performance is the result of milking the market for the good of the company—and not making a contribution to the world. Business is not separate from life. The two are interwoven. It is a great mistake to think there's no bottom line in all this. Uninspired people are the most costly and dangerous expenses to your business.

Final thanks to my family:
Ma, Dee, Leigh and Kit,
Bill and Kay, Missy and Julie;

and to my faithful
officemates,
Smokey and Charlie.

www.interactskills.com

REFERENCES

Beattie, Geoffrey (2003). *Visible Thoughts: The New Psychology of Body Language.* New York: Routledge.

Boulogne, Duchenne C. (1990). The Mechanism of Human Facial Expression (R.A. Cutherbertson Trans.) Paris: Jules Renard. (Original work published 1862) Cambridge: Cambridge University Press.

Brenkert, G. G. (1998). Trust, morality, and international business. In C. Lane & R. Backman (Eds.) Trust Within and Between Organizations. New York: Oxford University Press.

Campbell, Susan (2001). *Getting Real. The Ten Truth Skills You Need to Live an Authentic Life.* Tiburon: H. J. Kramer.

Collins, Jim (2001). Level 5 Leadership: The Triumph of Humility and Fierce Resolve. Best of Harvard Business Review.

Covey, Stephen (1989). *The Seven Habits of Highly Effective People.* New York: Simon and Schuster.

Ekman, P. (1992). Facial Expression of Emotion. *Psychological Science*, pp 3, 34-38.

George, B., Sims, P., McLean, A. N., & Mayer, D. (2007) *Discovering Your Authentic Leadership.* Harvard Business Review, pp 129-138.

Gladwell, Malcom (2007). *Blink, The Power of Thinking Without Thinking.* New York: Little, Brown and Company.

Goldberg, Natalie (1986). *Writing Down the Bones, Freeing the Writer Within.* Boston: Random House.

Goleman, Daniel (1995). *Emotional Intelligence.* New York: Bantam Books.

Gruber, P. (2007). The Four Truths of the Storyteller. *Harvard Business Review*, pp 85, 52-59.

Greene, Richard (2002). *Words That Shook the World: 100 Years of Unforgettable Speeches and Events.* New York: Penguin Putnam.

Heath, C. & Heath D. (2007). *Made to Stick, Why Some Ideas Survive and Others Die.* New York: Random House.

Homer, Trevor (2006). *The Book of Origins.* London: Penguins Books.

Howell, E. M. (1999). The human moment at work. *Harvard Business Review*, pp 77, 64- 68.

Kramer, R. M. (1999) Trust and distrust in organizations: Emerging Perspectives, Enduring Questions. *Annual Review of Psychology*, pp 50, 569-598.

Lane, Bill (2008). *Jacked Up. The Inside Story of How Jack Welch Talked GE into Becoming The World's Greatest Company.* New York: McGraw-Hill.

Johnston, Paul D. (1994) Humility: A Survival Tool. *A Review of General Semantics.* 51, 2, 171.

Lane, C. (1998). Theories and issues in the study of trust. In C. Lane & R. Backman (Eds.) Trust within and between organizations: conceptual issues and empirical applications. (pp 1-30). New York: Oxford University Press.

Maguire, Jack (1998). *The Power of Personal Storytelling: Spinning Tales to Connect with Others.* New York: Jeremy P. Tarcher/Putnam.

Mehrabian, Albert (1970). *Tactics in Social Influence,* Englewood Cliffs, New Jersey: Prentice-Hall.

Miller, John (1998). *Legends, Women Who Have Changed the World.* Novato: New World Library.

Mishra, A. K. (1996). Organizational responses to crisis: The centrality of trust. In R. Kramer & T. Tyler (Eds.) Trust in organizations: Frontiers of theory and research. (pp 261-287). Newbury Park, CA: Sage.

Peters, Tom (2003). *Re-imagine! Business Excellence in a Disruptive Age.* New York: Dorling Kindersley Limited.

Punn, Laurie (2000). *Instant Persuasion: How to Change Your Words to Change Your Life.* New York: Penguin Books.

Reynolds, Garr (2008). *Presentation Zen: Simple Ideas on Presentation Design and Delivery.* Berkeley: New Riders.

Rocco, E. (1998, April). Trust breaks down in electronic context but can be repaired by some initial face-to-face contact. Paper presented at the Conference on Human Factors in Computing Systems, Los Angeles, CA.

Sawyer, C. R. (2002). Behavioral Inhibition and the Communication of Public Speaking State Anxiety. *Western Journal of Communication.* p 66.

Scott, Susan (2004). *Fierce Conversations: Achieving Success at Work and in Life One Conversation at a Time.* Berkley Trade.

Simmons, Annette (2001). *The Story Factor.* Cambridge: Basic Books.

Tharp, Twyla (2003) *The Creative Habit, Learn It and Use It for Life.* New York: Simon & Schuster.

Thomas, Marlo (2002). *The Right Words at the Right Time.* New York: Atria Books.

Ueland, Brenda (1938). *If You Want To Write: A Book about Art, Independence and Spirit.* Saint Paul: Graywolf Press, 1938.

Zohar, Danah (2005, Fall) Spiritually Intelligent Leadership: *Leader to Leader Journal,* p 38.

Please share your stories, and the
stories you've heard that left their mark.
We would love to hear from you (really).

SaySomethingReal@InteractSkills.com

Lou Solomon
Interact Skills LLC
1435 West Morehead Street, Studio 210
Charlotte, NC 28208
Phone 704.374.0423 Fax 704.374.0443
www.InteractSkills.com